STACK THE DECK

The Ultimate Resource On Effectively Preparing, Presenting and Selling

Todd J. Carey

Compass Ventures Publishing

4760 Preston Road
Suite 244-249
Frisco, TX 75034

First Compass Ventures Publishing Edition, 2008

Designed by Megan Long
Manufactured in the United States of America

ISBN *978-0-6152-0766-7*

Praise for

STACK THE DECK

by Todd J. Carey

"Todd Carey has written an outstanding go-to book for today's sales force. Not only has he equipped corporate professionals with a guide for success, but essentially for any individual with an interest in simple, effective presenting.

> -- Kathleen Katona, Vice President,
> Compass Ventures, L.L.C.

"**STACK THE DECK** will give you the edge! Todd Carey has created the essential sales presentation handbook for all modern selling professionals. Highly relevant, easy to understand and implement and loaded with practical techniques, Carey has created the quintessential presenters guide that every sales manager should provide to their sales organization. This book is a "must-read" for everyone who wants to maximize their R.O.P! (Return On Presentations)"

> -- Simon Crossley, Vice President of Sales

Praise for

STACK THE DECK

by Todd J. Carey

"Todd Carey has written the 'playbook' for the modern sales professional. **STACK THE DECK** ensures that your sales team is delivering crisp, punchy presentations that effectively move the prospect from listener to participant to customer. Do yourself a favor and put this book in the hands of anyone in your organization that will ever stand in front of a customer."

-- Scott Ross, President

"Todd Carey has produced a book that should be required reading for anyone who values effective presentations. No matter your field, **STACK THE DECK** will give you the tools that you need to take your preparation and presentations to new levels!"

-- Khris Kennedy, Lead Pastor, First Baptist Church of Prosper

Acknowledgment

I dedicate this book to my family and friends for their support, inspiration and being a constant source of encouragement. My strength and confidence comes from my Lord and Savior, Jesus Christ.

Hebrews 12:1

Table of Contents

Table of Contents (cont.)

STACK THE DECK

Introduction

What if I bet you $500 you could not pull an Ace from a standard deck of playing cards? Would you take it? If you are a serious gambler you may consider it, but if you are a rational person with an adverse reaction to losing money, you probably will turn me down. Why? It's basic math. You have 4 cards to win and I have the other 48 since there are only 4 cards of each type in a standard 52 card deck. Your odds of pulling an Ace are 1 in 13 (not very good in case you were wondering). However, if I change the bet and now offer you $500 to pull an Ace from 5 cards *you select* in a 52 card deck, would you take that bet? You would be foolish not to since I never specified which 5 cards you could or could not choose. You now have the power to control most of the variables and gain an advantage *which is a recurring theme throughout this book.* Your best combination, of course, would be 4 Aces and a random card giving you 4 cards to win to my one. This improves your odds to 4 out of 5. By stacking the deck in your favor you have given yourself much better odds for success.

Employing this type of strategy as it relates to presenting and selling can mean the difference between winning and losing. Unfortunately, most salespeople choose not to and prefer to take their chances. They arrive with their standard presentation deck (slides) and worn out sales pitch used on every prospect in recent memory. They have no road map or guidelines for their meeting or any predetermined goals. As a result, they can't tell you what a successful meeting will be at the end of a presentation, before it ever begins. This unfortunate compilation of errors is the downfall of most salespeople who foolishly forego leveraging every tool and resource available to them to prepare, present and sell successfully. Learning to Stack The Deck starts with the most basic and vital component of a sound sales strategy: preparation.

There are many facets of preparation and most salespeople will tell you they always prepare for meetings. When I ask them to define "preparation", common answers are delivery, rehearsing, working on content, confirming meeting times and attendees, etc. We will discuss all of these items in more detail throughout this book, but a sales presenter must go far beyond working on timing, speaking posture and eye contact. These traits equate to mere gift wrapping on the total package needed to close a sale. Although they cannot be overlooked, they do not properly prepare a *sales* person to give a *sales* presentation. The misconception that these techniques are what make a sales presenter effective is why sales presenting is often crammed inside public speaking resources.

There are numerous types of presentations we could discuss like training, seminars, lectures, orientations and others. We will only focus on sales, but many of the fundamentals and techniques in this book can be applied to any presenting effort. There are very good resources available to become a more effective public speaker, but if you are researching ways to improve your sales numbers through better fundamentals and sales presenting, good luck in finding that book until now. Most resources in this area help you make your presentation more enjoyable and entertaining, but not sell your product better. People love to hear stories and watch well orchestrated presentations, but time and again, both the stories and presenters are forgettable. Don't spend time honing your skills to be a polished and exciting presenter at the expense of not incorporating sound sales principles. If you are not prepared to sell your product and can't guide the meeting to close the deal, reminding yourself not to jingle pocket change won't help. You are presenting your product to prospective buyers in a sales meeting. So simple question: did you sell something or not? Making an audience laugh and enjoy your presentation is good, but getting them to buy what you are selling is even better. Apply the principles in this book and you will discover confidence through your subject matter and preparation efforts that will allow your personality to be one of your greatest assets, instead of the only thing you have to rely on. The goal is to become a confident presenter and an expert salesperson. That is a powerful and profitable combination.

We will cover what proper preparation is in chapter one, but it is useful to first understand why salespeople apply minimal effort or skip this important step. The primary catalyst to this behavior is the common saying that, "Sales is a numbers game." Simply put, more calls and more presentations equal more sales. What this statement is really referring to is choosing quantity over quality as the main sales performance metric. While I will not dispute that constant activity is proven to drive numbers, if it is mainly how sales effectiveness is measured, it has an adverse effect on the quality standards and performance of the sales team. Salespeople try to stay busy jumping from account to account looking for the quick win to make quota. They try to fit into a system instead of developing dynamic sales

The selling culture today is a mixed bag of motivational tapes, simple math equations and garage sale bartering.

skills that will allow them to fully develop quality opportunities and relationships. To compensate for this flawed model, sales managers will infuse outside consultants, team building events and new sales books to bolster sales productivity and results. Believing these activities are what truly drive effectiveness, the cycle continues with managers wondering why they cannot get their team on track. The failure is imminent so when the latest "self-help sales" program falls apart, it is dismissed as just another excuse to "get back to basics" and reinvent the numbers game again. As a result, the selling culture today is a mixed bag of motivational tapes, simple math equations and garage sale bartering. If you can't close the deal after the initial truck load of features and benefits dumped on the boardroom table, it turns into a race of how fast you can out-discount your competition. Sound familiar?

There is a better way to present and sell effectively and to find it, we begin by looking deeper into the word "sales." If you look up "sales" in the dictionary, it is defined simply as "the transfer of ownership." If you examine this definition for a moment, it is interesting to note that it makes no mention of money changing hands. It implies only that something was previously owned then transferred to a new owner. If we insert a salesperson and customer into this definition as our transfer points, we get the definition of sales as "the transfer of ownership from a salesperson to the customer." Even with the smallest amount of deductive reasoning we can conclude

> **Before the customer can take ownership, a salesperson has to own what they are selling.**

that since the customer now owns something that was previously owned by someone else, the previous owner had to be the salesperson.

Clearly then before the customer can take ownership, a salesperson has to own what they are selling. Not physical possession as the traditional definition would suggest. I define sales ownership as, "The ability to utilize product knowledge in a way that makes features flexible and relevant to the prospect in order to make the sale."

The number of good salespeople who never take the time to research their own product first before attempting to sell it to someone else is extraordinary. They breeze through initial sales trainings or glance over product and customer information. All in an effort to get out to the field as quickly as possible since the commission clock is running. As we will see, owning your product is not a "check the box" process nor should it be treated like a test cramming exercise. True ownership is having a comprehensive product understanding and the capability to adapt it to fit your customer's needs. If you cannot successfully align your product with what your buyer is looking for, your sales meeting probably won't involve any sales.

It is important to note that we will also discuss how to strategically integrate this process while creating forward momentum in a new sales role. One of the major reasons why sales professionals skip this effort is that they are pressured and expected to train themselves while immediately prospecting for new opportunities. Unfortunately, most sales organizations do not allocate enough time for new hires to properly acclimate themselves to their new company, product and culture.

Once you have product ownership, you now have to transfer it to your buyer. As we will see in Stack The Deck, this effort involves introducing them to what you have to offer and training them to be an expert on your product. We will go into great detail on how this process works, but you will never get this far during your meeting if you are not confident and convincing. Even if you have an impressive product or service, a terrible presentation will encourage your audience to check email during the meeting to feel productive. Worse yet, you leave the buyer wanting to know more about who else is bidding for their business.

I have given thousands of presentations ranging from small internal meetings to large scale venues in front of thousands of people. Some were meant to secure sales and new business; others were for strategic partnerships or sales training. However, regardless of the presentation type, the common theme among my most successful presentations was the right kind of preparation. I not only knew my material, I knew my audience and how I was going to make them care about what I had to say. I knew my product and its relevance to them. I knew the points of influence and what I was going to ask for at the end. Most importantly, I knew what success looked like when I walked off the stage or out of the boardroom. Preparation is the key to gaining this knowledge base and being able to control the inconsistent elements of a presentation like audience feedback, technical difficulties and time shortage to name a few.

These tools will empower you to excel in almost any situation with minimal preparation before each meeting.

To illustrate this point further, compare a sales presentation to a team's game plan and playbook in the National Football League (NFL). The actual 60 minute game is a culmination of tireless preparation, scouting, strategies, real time adjustments and play calling to attack the other team's weaknesses. How successful would a NFL team be if they prepared for every opponent the same way with the same plays and never adjusted for anyone? I would wager that you would not see a winning record anytime soon.

What happens then when the prepared game plan is not successful? Coaches will change the plays, adjust at half time for weaknesses in their strategy or unforeseen injuries and come out with a new plan in the third quarter. Incredibly, most sales people do not have a similar, flexible approach for their sales meetings. They show up with basically the same deck (presentation slides), rename the file, present their product the exact same way with a, "See anything you like?" question at the end. How can you ever achieve relevance to your customers by using a deck and presentation strategy that is not tailored to your buyer's needs and/or reflects all of your discussions and research done before you meet?

Some traditional sales people may believe it is unrealistic to recreate presentation decks and change approaches for every meeting. They have been doing it their way for years and they can't see a reason to change. These traditionalists may be in your company or even better, your competition. Either way, it is this attitude that leaves them vulnerable to an aggressive and prepared competitor tearing them apart one deal at a time.

Stack The Deck methods do not take as much time as they may appear. There is an additional time commitment compared to changing file names and the date on the intro page, but success requires more effort and prospects both demand and deserve it. We will discuss techniques that greatly reduce preparation and rehearsal time utilizing Adaptive Product Knowledge and a Product Presence. These tools will empower you to excel in almost any situation with minimal preparation before each meeting.

However, no matter the amount of preparation and research, you will never have the perfect message every time. Only by owning your product and presentation will you be able to adjust and be successful in any circumstance, with any audience and any content. Preparing for everything, knowing your product and having both relevance and a connection to your audience is what it means to Stack The Deck.

There are three main sections in this book: Prepare, Present and Sell as outlined in the diagram below:

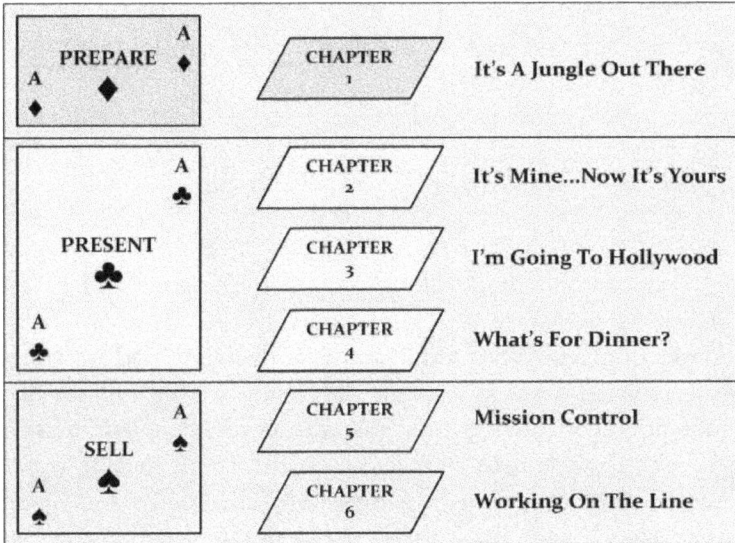

PREPARE ◆	CHAPTER 1	It's A Jungle Out There
PRESENT ♣	CHAPTER 2	It's Mine...Now It's Yours
	CHAPTER 3	I'm Going To Hollywood
	CHAPTER 4	What's For Dinner?
SELL ♠	CHAPTER 5	Mission Control
	CHAPTER 6	Working On The Line

Here is a summary of each chapter:

Chapter 1 -- It's A Jungle Out There

We will discuss the most important ingredient to not just surviving, but excelling at presentations: preparation. Sound preparation techniques and principles like completing a Risk Assessment and conducting a Pre-Presentation call will remove most of the unknowns. This will produce a high level of presenter confidence that you can handle anything that is coming your way.

Chapter 2 -- It's Mine...Now It's Yours

You will always enter the presentation as the product or service expert. You must execute and be convincing in this role or the customer will not allow you to mold what you have to sell into what they need. Developing Adaptive Product Knowledge (APK) and a Product Presence will produce a powerful combination and help you train your buyer to be a product expert. Once you have achieved this milestone, you are well on your way to winning the business.

Chapter 3 -- I'm Going To Hollywood

In your continued development as a prepared and polished presenter, character development is crucial. You can create a connection with your audience with charisma and personality. Unfortunately, these are the last traits to be visible to an audience. You have to get past the nerves, environment, and product alignment to start feeling comfortable and be yourself. Actors refer to this as, "getting into character" and "playing their role." In case you were wondering, your role is to convince and to sell.

Chapter 4 –What's For Dinner?

You are guide, not the guided. As the sales presenter and the product expert in the room, you must know where you are going. More importantly your audience has to believe and trust you enough to follow. It comes down to assuming the pro-active role, gaining their trust and owning the important information. Use it to be the influencer and determine the outcome.

Chapter 5 -- Mission Control

We will discuss why you don't want to present first in a sales meeting. A well organized interview session with your buyer in the beginning of a presentation will give you a firm advantage heading into your time in front of the room. Through sound interview techniques, you will be able to retain the power, which in a sales context, is more like influence. Stack The Deck will give you the ability to suggest, control and navigate your way to the close. Influence is present throughout a sales meeting and it needs to stay on your side if you want to be the winner.

Chapter 6 – Working On The Line

In much the same way that Henry Ford produced Model Ts from an assembly line, your build up to the close should follow the same progression. Your tactics before, during and after your presentation will determine how successful you are in winning. Too many sales presenters attempt to "wing it" at the end of their meeting using too much emotion and not enough mechanics. A strong close is produced from having a solid plan and *earning the right* to ask for the business.

Critical Success Factors (CSF)

Throughout Stack The Deck, there are special sections called Critical Success Factors (CSF). These are tools, resources, recommendations, and discussion points that draw specific emphasis on chapter content. The format is relatively simple. First, there is a numbered and detailed list for each CSF in larger bold and italic type. Then the individual points that need additional discussion will follow.

STACK the DECK

CSF Summary

1. **Don't Roll The Dice**

   Constructing a Risk Assessment (Chapter 1)

2. **Scouting Your Opponents**

   Pre-meeting Call (Chapter 1)

3. **Game Time Decisions**

   Adaptive Product Knowledge (APK) (Chapter 2)

4. **Playing The Game**

   Character development before and during your presentation

   (Chapter 3)

5. **Hedging Your Bet**

   Content and meeting strategy (Chapter 4)

6. **The Odds On Favorite**

   Presentation influence (Chapter 5)

7. **Bet, Raise and All-In**

   Assembly line close (Chapter 6)

A
♦
PREPARE
♦
A
♦

A
♣
PRESENT
♣
A
♣

A
♠
SELL
♠
A
♠

A
♥
CONFIDENCE
♥
A
♥

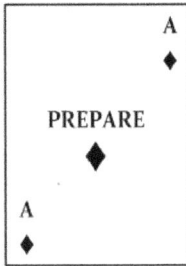

One final element of Stack The Deck are the two Aces you will see at the beginning of each chapter. The two card theme is in honor of one of my favorite games, Texas Hold'em.

To be successful at the game of Poker, you must have skill, strategy, steady nerves and know how to balance your emotions in all kinds of situations to be a consistent winner. Sounds a lot like sales.

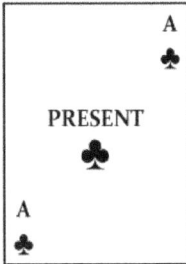

A Texas Hold'em poker game begins with each player being dealt two cards. They are referred to as player's "starting hand" and a pair of Aces is the most powerful starting hand possible. Then after several rounds of betting, a total of five "community" cards are dealt face up on the table. These cards can be used by all the players with their own two cards to make the best hand possible. The odds of starting with Aces is rare (1 in 221), but the good news is that in this book, you get dealt two Aces six times in a row.

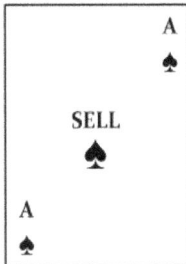

The first Ace will tell you whether you are in the Prepare, Present or Sell sections. The second Ace, the Ace of Confidence, is included in every chapter of this book since confidence is always needed in every sales situation. In fact, the word confidence is mentioned almost 40 times in Stack The Deck. Confidence, combined with the techniques and strategies in this book make you virtually unbeatable. OK, let's get started…

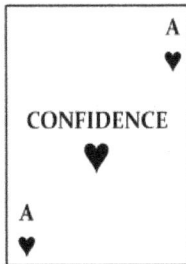

Chapter 1

It's A Jungle Out There

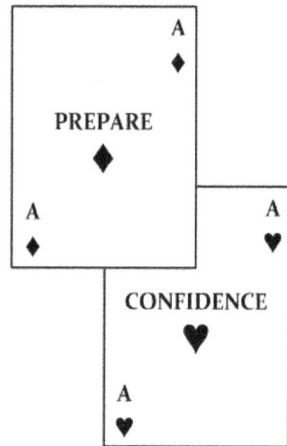

"If I always appear prepared, it is because before entering an undertaking, I have meditated long and have foreseen what might occur. It is not genius that reveals to me suddenly and secretly what I should do in circumstances unexpected by others; it is thought and preparation."

Napoleon Bonaparte

If you surveyed any salesperson and asked them what they feel is the most important element of any sales presentation, you will undoubtedly get some very strong opinions (since everyone is an expert, including myself). I conduct this brief interview with almost every salesperson I meet. The general responses of, "Delivery, making eye contact, not talking over the audience, easy to read slides, arriving prepared" are a sampling of what I hear. Obviously all of these items are important, but there is one that precedes them all. As mentioned in the introduction, it is the simplest but most critical to any successful presentation: preparation.

The first step to Stack The Deck is to develop a systematic approach to your preparation efforts. Forget the old adage, "Practice makes perfect." Vince Lombardi said it best with, "Practice does not make perfect. Only perfect practice makes perfect." If you want to yield consistent results, you must follow a routine and structure in preparing before a presentation. This is the premise for the Stack The Deck preparation model. Let's face it, presenting is hard enough and complicating it with the stress of the unknown or the absent minded doesn't improve your odds.

> **If you want to yield consistent results, you must follow a routine and structure in preparing before a presentation.**

You can find an excellent representation of this model in action if you ever watch a professional golfer. In any tournament and in any situation, almost every pro golfer has developed a pre shot routine. In the beginning, they will gauge the conditions, lie of the ball, risk, hazards, distance, wind and so on. Then they visualize the swing, shot needed and see themselves executing it to perfection with the ball in flight. Regardless of what is at stake, the score or conditions, a professional golfer will go through these progressions until they are confident they can make the shot. Many experts and psychologists agree that visualizing success positively influences results.

Presenters need to have this same mindset to always approach their meetings and presentations the same way. Visualize then execute. In doing so, it helps eliminate variables, creates consistency and builds speaker confidence.

So let's discuss a pre-shot routine in terms of a presentation. Every successful salesperson should have a progression or checklist they go through to make sure they have everything needed. Not just in terms of presentation material, but unforeseen factors like the environment, attendees, projector or other equipment, etc. How about an Internet connection or scheduling subject matter experts on call? Do you need application demonstrations? If you sell technology, you know how critical those last items can be. For example, I have spent some time in the mobile solutions marketplace involved with products like Personal Data Assistants (PDAs) and wireless software. It always amazes me how some sales reps can show up to a sales presentation and not have charged the handhelds they were trying to sell. Seriously, just plug them in the night before so the buyer can actually see the devices working. Is that too much to ask if you are selling handheld technology? Furthermore, if a handheld crashed while giving a demo they neglected to bring a back up device as if the one they had was the only one in the universe.

You need to consider every possible need, request, opportunity and potential failure to be ready for a sales presentation.

Regardless of the industry you sell in, you can probably think of countless examples of poor preparation. It produces poor results and the buyer will never accept any excuses for wasting their time.

I will certainly label myself as an optimist, but I have pessimistically named my pre-presentation routine as my Risk Assessment. "Murphy's Law" is never far away when you are presenting and trying to sell something. I have shown up for huge presentations having just shut my laptop off when my plane landed and then not able to turn it on again 20 minutes later. Trapped inside were all my slides, material and demo tools. Good thing I had a back up plan in place for my presentation and Internet connectivity.

Quick Tip: Email the presentation to yourself and the others on your presenting team before the meeting. This turns your team's email inbox into a virtual safe store of information if you have an email account you can access from the Web. That way if your laptop goes down and you have an Internet connection, you can log on and launch your presentation from any laptop with Microsoft PowerPoint.

You need to consider every possible need, request, opportunity and potential failure to be ready for a sales presentation. A Risk Assessment is a checklist you will create that is meant to produce consistency in both your preparation and delivery performance. Simply put, you need to know what you are getting into before you show up for the meeting.

This checklist should be a simple form designed for quick reference that won't take long to complete. Again, we are all short on time so make it easy on yourself. For every meeting, I will take 10 minutes, close my door and visualize the entire presentation from arrival to departure. I then create a list or modify an old one to meet my latest requirements.

STACK THE DECK

Critical Success Factor (CSF) Don't Roll The Dice

Constructing a Risk Assessment

1. Create a quick checklist for all resources <u>you will supply</u> for the presentation (i.e., laptop, power cord, demonstration tools, printed presentations, etc.)

2. Create a quick checklist for all resources the prospect or <u>host will supply</u> (i.e., internet connection, projector, large or small meeting room, etc.)

3. List all potential problems and/or risks and how they will affect the presentation (i.e., directions to meeting location, poor or failed internet, no projector, missing attendees)

4. List all work-arounds for all items listed in #3 and presentation impact if any

5. List the next steps to be achieved from your presentation and points of risk

(examples and more resources are available at www.stackitonline.com and the Appendix)

It is important to note that the Risk Assessment does not have to be a long and laborious process. It is meant to get you started and remove most of the unknown and control variables so you can concentrate on your presentation. Above is a general checklist and adjust these items as time allows or as needed. However, make sure you have covered all your points of risk.

You need to take a different perspective on defining a presentation. I view a presentation as an agreement or an understanding between you and your audience that they will meet and listen to you at a predetermined time slot. There is an implied promise they will pay attention and you will bring an informative and valuable message. In sales, when you book your first appointment with a prospect, you have reached your first agreement…congratulations.

Once this agreement is consummated with a meeting planner, what happens next is inexplicable. Most prospects never get a call back from the salesperson before the meeting to confirm the agenda, attendees or discuss changes to the project since their last discussion. At most, the agenda or attendees are confirmed by administrative assistants or at the last minute by the sales lead via email or phone. If anything proactively is sent from the sales lead, it is a, "Let me know if you would like to add anything else" type communication. A customer is never going to play their hand and give you all of their buying points and topics of interest or concern upfront. A buyer loves to keep the sales team off balance and ambush them with tough questions. This flawed approach referenced above leaves you exposed to attack and trust me, they're coming fully armed.

> **A buyer loves to keep the sales team off balance and ambush them with tough questions.**

This simple communication between you and the decision makers (or at the very least the organizers, but not the administrative staff) to have them sign off on what will be covered is our second Critical Success Factor (CSF). By getting a unanimous agreement from both your staff and the prospect, you create accountability to what will take place and the content discussed.

STACK THE DECK

Critical Success Factor (CSF)

Scouting Your Opponents   *Pre-meeting Call*

1. *Confirm meeting agenda and attendees*

2. *Introduce new items or topics to gauge interest and/or define scope*

3. *Try to raise product objections and encourage feedback by discussing potential issues on the call BEFORE the meeting*

4. *Investigate whether or not anyone else should attend or be affected by a decision to move forward*

5. *Discuss your team members with the prospect and explain why they are attending*

6. *Confirm logistics and any possibility for additional activities like private break out sessions, lunch, golf, etc.*

7. *Create the meeting agenda and ask for a distribution list. (This also gives you the list to send out an immediate follow up email after the meeting)*

(examples and more resources are available at www.stackitonline.com and the Appendix)

The size and importance of your meeting will determine what points are discussed and/or omitted from the call. It may be just a simple one-on-one meeting to briefly review and talk with an already motivated prospect. However, it may be a large meeting with important people and busy calendars, so you want to make sure you have done your homework and have the right message prepared.

For this reason, I need to highlight point **#1:** *Confirm meeting agenda and attendees* and focus on the "confirming attendee" reference. This can be done either via phone or email, but simply filling out a seating chart is not the purpose of this exercise. It is in your best interest to find out as much as you can about your audience through the traditional channels to create relevance to your product.

It is also possible to research your meeting attendees through other venues. With today's free flowing information highways, you can find out just about anything you want on just about anyone. Use this to your advantage (hint: avoid extortion, incriminating photographs or blackmail) by focusing on press releases, bios, published interviews and links from company websites and other sources. You will be much more effective when answering questions and finding alignment with specific individuals in your audience if you know something about them and their company. If you can discover their positions on say technology platforms or political views, you can avoid potential verbal land mines and comments meant to be humorous that may get you in trouble. Again, this takes a little time and planning, but the payoff is potentially huge in comparison to the effort.

An alternative viewpoint to consider is often overlooked. How did your meeting get scheduled? Most of the time your "champion" or point of contact schedules the meeting at your request and pulls in the attendees on their side. Their name is now on the meeting as the internal "organizer." They have inadvertently made themselves accountable internally for the success or failure of the meeting. What happens if you fall apart in the presentation and the content misses the mark? The attendees feel like they have wasted their time and will not only have contempt for you, but for the person that dragged them there in the first place. Use this to your advantage to ask them questions about those attending and what needs to be discussed. They have a vested interest in the meetings success so they should be willing to help you.

Here's an important point to remember: from the first moment you meet any prospect you are being evaluated. If you ask for an executive level audience, you better be an executive level quality presenter. Most buyers will not put their corporate standing at risk for a vendor they do not believe will be effective in front of their peers and executive management.

Discovering problems with time to respond is much better than getting attacked with no place to hide.

Most of the other points are straightforward except for **#3:** *Try to raise product objections and encourage feedback by discussing potential issues on the call BEFORE the meeting*. This action will take some skill and time to develop properly, but it will be your most useful tool in arriving prepared. The strategy is to draw out possible "show stoppers" and major objections before you are onsite with the customer. This way, if they do divulge something that needs to be addressed, you can prepare responses and create work-arounds without being directly in front of the buyer.

Some of the topics you can discuss are buyer requirements or preferences that may already be established. For example, technical preferences, third party vendor contracts, existing supplier relationships or recent related purchases to your product or service may all be information you can gather before you arrive. You have to prepare for both your presentation and your buyer. It is important to note that this is not done exclusively on the pre-meeting call. As we will see, it should be a constant effort to draw out objections before and after you arrive.

If there are potential pitfalls, do your best to discover those before you get there. Discovering problems with time to respond is much better than getting attacked with no place to hide. This approach reminds me of a story when my younger brother and I had the brilliant idea of going hornet hunting.

We quietly crept up to their enormous hive. It was about three and a half feet in circumference and from about 30 feet away you could hear the hornets hum like a Panzer tank waiting for you to show yourself. I will tell you if you have never come face to face with one of these flying bullets of pain, save yourself the experience or it will haunt you the rest of your days. Nevertheless, we were young, dumb and brave and my brother had the genius idea of trying to take out the base by hurling half rotten pears from a distance. Unfortunately, aged pears provide for very poor projectiles and they leave you with two choices: go home or get closer. As two fearless grade school warriors, we chose the latter. So with every step toward that hive of death, I was convincing myself I had lived a good life to the age of 10 and anything that happened from here on out would be a bonus.

We were launching pears with the rifled accuracy of a fire extinguisher when my brother suddenly breaks into a maniacal sprint. At full speed he unleashes a mashed pear bunker buster right through the hive's main entrance. It was an impressive throw, but what happens next is somewhat of a blur. I was somewhere between experiencing screeching fear for my brother and self-preservation as a black cloud of kamikaze dive bombers rose from their destroyed hive. If you have never seen and heard an eight year old boy run like a cheetah and scream like a girl, you are missing out on one of the funniest scenes life has to offer. He threw off his coat when they peppered it with stingers and he barely made it out of there alive.

I tell you that story as an analogy to note the similarity of drawing out your objections to your product before your meeting so you can react to them on your terms, not during a full retreat and shedding clothes in the process. Interview as many people as you can, try to address potential problems on the pre-conference call, do whatever it takes to gain an edge. Discovering a customer's objections for the first time during a presentation is like hurling half rotten pears at a hornet's nest. I'm sure you can survive it, but there are better ways to spend your time-especially if your career depends on it.

> **Interview as many people as you can, try to address potential problems on the pre-conference call, do whatever it takes to gain an edge.**

Another advantage of knowing your customer's objections in advance is that it allows you to bring them up first during your presentation before your buyer does. In this case, whoever talks first, wins. If you offer up an objection, you remove the power from the customer and it becomes a *point of discussion*. If they raise the objection on their own, it is now something for you to overcome and a *true objection*. It now must be dealt with while the buyer wields their heavy hammer of discontent at your product.

Now let's look at an example of how this works *during* a sales presentation. Suppose you are selling sanitizing chemicals and cleaners to restaurants. You know that most of these companies already have a long term supplier and that will be your largest objection. How do you counter that objection? One possibility may be to offer an incentive on their first purchase with you. You may choose to calculate their discount based on a percentage of what they have already spent with your competitor this year. BEFORE they say "we already have someone that supplies that to us" make this offer along with the reasons why your product is better.

This may sound like common sense and you may be saying to yourself, "I am already prepared to hear those types of objections." If you are an experienced sales person you probably have a canned response. However, are you the aggressor or do you wait to hear the objection until you spring into action? There is a monumental difference between properly responding to an objection and initiating the topic. You are relinquishing power to the prospect in allowing them to think they have you cornered and figured out. Throw them off balance and take a different path than 99% of the sales people they meet.

I have included a brief list of some of the more common objections you may face in bold text and my suggested points of discussion in quotations. Below the discussion points, I have offered some additional comments on that objection. Again, if you expect these types of statements, you are the one that needs to bring them up, not your buyer.

1. **"Your product is not specific enough to our industry."**

   Possible response: "We have a customized approach for each company and do not force you to fit into our product."

   Every customer wants to feel like they are spending money for the perfect fit. If your product is not specific enough to their industry, you cannot change that overnight. Instead, focus on the value that makes you different in your approach to customizing and delivering your product to meet their specific needs.

2. **"Your company is not big enough for us."**

Possible response: "We are a smaller and more flexible company without the layers of politics and bureaucracy found in larger organizations."

Possible response: "We are a small, but a well funded company with the resources to support an enterprise class opportunity. We routinely submit our financials as part of our product quote."

This is one of the more difficult objections to overcome. In larger deals, there is no doubt that bigger companies have the advantage due to the security it offers the buyer. Most of the time, your buyers are simply employees wanting to make the right product choice, but also keep their job. Going bigger is not always best, but it feels safe to the buyer. Create this type of security on your own outside of strictly reviewing financials by discussing your past successes and why you can be trusted.

3. **"Your product/service is not established enough in the industry."**

Possible response: "We have a focused product development team and are over committing resources to providing support and attention to our early adopting customers."

Buyers love to hear that you are committing a lot of resources to their project. More resources on your side generally equals less work for them which is an advantage to selecting your company. Also, make sure they understand that you know how to manage and deliver what you are selling and you will not quit until they are satisfied.

4. **"Your competitor is much cheaper."**

Possible response: "On average, we are more expensive than most of our competitors. There are valuable features we choose to include that most do not such as …" or " Our service staff that supports you and our products set us apart…"

How do you want to be compared to your competition? If they are selecting on price and price alone, you need to convince them they are using the wrong decision metrics. If you don't challenge their thought process, you are just another vendor submitting a quote. Anytime a buyer makes their decision solely on price, it is anyone's game to win. You need to tip the playing field in your favor. If you are more expensive, you must be able to justify the difference. Itemize it out before you get to your meeting and begin offering these differences before they start squeezing you on cost.

I suggest taking good notes on your pre-meeting calls and bringing these notes to your presentation to add to them during the meeting. This way, during the close you can go back and reference the value you have already established and it doesn't look like you are trying to play catch up. If you start trying to make your case after they begin beating you up on price, it will devalue those items and damage your image. We will discuss this in more detail and how to properly close your presentation in chapter six.

Setting the meeting agenda in reference to **#7:** *Create the meeting agenda and ask for a distribution list.* This effort involves a lot more sales skill than simply deciding the amount of time needed to present and what content to bring. I have been a part of some very large meetings where the sales lead would leave the meeting feeling ambushed because either someone new attended or a new objection or topic was introduced. Salespeople have no one to blame but themselves for failure due to lack of pre-presentation planning. If you are leading the charge, it is your responsibility to make sure everything goes according to plan. Whether it is a casual one on one introductory meeting or a huge summit with the big guns, you have to be prepared for anything. Think of yourself as a walking success insurance policy that can be used or canceled at anytime. Although you will never be able to predict the future, not running risk assessments and preparing for what else could be discussed other than your agenda can be detrimental to your sales health. This costly error occurs so often in sales and is the epicenter of the following story that demonstrates just how damaging missing this point can be.

Our company had been under fire from our investors for missing our sales forecast for the third straight quarter. So when we received the call that we were chosen to be one of two potential vendors in a Fortune 100 company's RFP process, we were both elated and relieved. We felt we had all the skills necessary and the supporting product to be great, all we needed was the time and place to showcase our talents. With the missed forecasts and grumpy investors, this was a critical meeting for our software integration company.

We had an audience with the executive team and a chance for a huge win for the company. We were also chasing the promise of that much needed commission check. We had diligently prepared for weeks in anticipation for this presentation and blocked out our calendars leading up to the appointment to make sure we were focused and ready. Our entire sales team couldn't wait to get off the plane, present the slides, close the deal and go celebrate the win. Cautious optimism gave way to spending the commission checks after we arrived on their campus and knew there was a budget item in there somewhere for us. Of course, there was pressure to perform. We had posted this deal on the sales pipeline as closing this quarter and the customer had already given us some excellent buying signals. We rehearsed and revised the presentation for what seemed like a thousand times and were overly confident we could get this done.

In addition to having one of the best presentation decks we had ever created, we were sponsored by their VP of Sales and had several preliminary conference calls to introduce our product and services to some other important company influencers. We also had some relationships inside the organization through our own personal networks who helped us prepare. This due diligence was to ensure we had the proper message and confirm we were the right fit to move naturally into discussing implementation timelines and contracts. We did not get sponsorship from these other influencers nor could we use their names in the presentation, but they confidentially guided us with "insider" information so we thought we had all of the data needed to be successful.

Our VP of Sales lead the way and was absolutely prepared to deliver our presentation complete with a killer value proposition. Our business development team was in place and waiting for the time to jump in and support him with any specific expertise needed. We had choreographed the slides during the presentation for the team to provide analysis and commentaries making us look sophisticated and prepared. Needless to say, we had all of the pieces required to complete the sales puzzle. All we had to do was show up and execute, but what happened next would change the way I have approached and prepared for every presentation since.

We arrived early enough to make sure we had time to set up and display the presentation and be organized when the prospects walked in. The "C" team arrived on time, thanked us for coming in and asked to get started right away. Our sales lead stood up, introduced the team and was about 5 slides into a 50 slide deck when they seemed unsettled and asked to stop the presentation. They told us that we were too far ahead in the slide content and needed to back up for the benefit of a few new attendees that had not been involved in previous discussions. It was noted that they would have some kind of buy in on this purchase since their business units were going to be affected.

At this point, panic was probably a good word to describe our camp since we had built and timed the entire presentation to drive toward one goal, the sale. We had not prepared any recap or follow up slides, no time was designated for a discussion regarding the past accomplishments or a documented timeline provided for the benefit of anyone not previously involved. We could not bring them up to speed on our progress in an organized and controlled fashion, so instead we were scrambling to pull out notes and speaking from memory on how we got to this meeting. As a result, we opened ourselves up to criticism from the new attendees for not properly seeking approval from all business units involved and moving too quickly.

Not having the supporting data and dates readily available left us open for attack with little resistance. The fact that no one accounted for a recap discussion or came prepared to accommodate such a request seemed completely illogical and inexplicable. Nonetheless, we were now forced into a very weak position looking unprepared. We had surrendered all power to the customer as a result of one request 10 minutes into a scripted three hour presentation.

To make matters worse, our new attendees were official "grandstanders" taking the opportunity to fire questions aimed at the presenter that were meant to be adversarial in hopes of impressing the higher ranks. Our attempt at a quick recap rapidly evolved into a train wreck with the new attendees asking pointed questions relevant only to their area of expertise and poking holes in our value proposition. The ship really began to sink when the "C" level team began shaking their heads in agreement with some of the points raised and began to ask new questions of their own. Now the recap turned into a re-sell and we were clearly not prepared to start from the beginning and close this deal in two and a half hours. Panic now turned to disappointment, which gave way to panic again when we realized not only were we in danger of losing control of the meeting, we were close to losing a potential customer.

Right on queue to that epiphany, another blow hit with painful devastation with the statement from the customer, "By the way, we know you have traveled to get here and we appreciate that, but we had a very important meeting come up this afternoon and we are going to have to end 30 minutes earlier than our scheduled time." All of our preparation and rehearsing and the best deck we had ever created was now rendered officially worthless. It was no longer a general feeling of panic, it was more like, "Let's go find a bridge and all jump off together. That way we won't have to report back on how our biggest sales meeting to date flopped from the wrong kind of preparation." The visions of celebrating and closing a high profile account in this meeting turned into, "How do we salvage an opportunity with this company enough to have some positive next steps?"

I am pleased to tell you that we did in fact save the account and this story had a happy ending. Blowing up a meeting of this magnitude puts you in a very compromised position and consider yourself fortunate if you get another chance. Lucky for us, the wonderful time known as the dot.com era afforded a technology company a few failures before they had to get it right. However, once in recovery mode, you no longer have the ability to drive all by yourself and need to atone for your mistakes. So we systematically went after every attendee in the room that day and contacted them individually. We collected their core agenda items and why this purchase was important to them and their business unit. Some had profit and loss concerns, others had more application and technical issues. We used our negative as a positive to extract information that would otherwise be carefully guarded by beginning our requests with, "In order to avoid what happened before, tell me…" After our interviews were done, we aggregated all of our data to reconstruct the value proposition for the new buying committee. With their requirements now being met, we rescheduled and resold them from start to finish. A sales person's job is not just to convince and to sell, it is to properly prepare and manage events before, during and after a sales presentation.

Completing a Risk Assessment and conducting a Pre-Presentation Call are absolutes if you are going to be ready for anything. As sales presenters, we are constantly judged and measured. A Stack The Deck preparation effort is critical in producing confidence in both presenter and presentation and it will remove most of the unknown that you should be able to control. More importantly, it enables you to focus on convincing them your product is the one they should buy which is the reason you are there in the first place.

Chapter 1 Review

1. Presentation Pre-shot Routine

Every successful salesperson should have their own system and metrics by which to measure themselves. Follow a process where you visualize your presentation, goals achieved and what success looks like when the meeting ends. This will lead you to a consistent effort and more importantly, a proven standard to gauge success or failure.

2. Constructing a Risk Assessment

A Risk Assessment should be used to remove most of the "unknown" in your pre-presentation planning and reduce anxiety. Reducing variables and risk along with giving you more time to focus on your presentation is a worthwhile activity. It does not have to be a long list, but it needs to be thorough. Review your list after each presentation to make sure you did not miss anything or to remove extra items that are not needed.

3. Pre-meeting Call To Confirm Agenda

This simple communication between you and the decision makers (or at the very least the organizers) to have them sign off on what will be covered is vital. By getting a unanimous agreement from both your staff and the prospect, you create accountability *for both vendor and buyer* to what will take place and the content discussed.

4. Avoid The Hammer Of Discontent

Regardless of your type of product, you should know the areas that most customers object to and all about your competition. Use this knowledge to your advantage. If you offer up an objection, you remove the power from the customer and it becomes a *point of discussion.* If they raise the objection on their own, it is now something for you to overcome and a *true objection* that must be dealt with on their terms.

Chapter 2

It's Mine...Now It's Yours

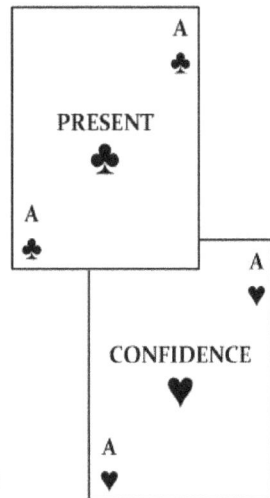

"The salesman knows nothing of what he is selling save that he is charging a great deal too much for it."

Oscar Wilde, late 19th century

We have already defined sales as the transfer of ownership. To really understand this definition, you have to ask yourself, "Do I know enough about what I am selling that I can successfully present and align it to any audience, in any situation?" If you can't walk into a conference room and lead the discussion of your product and establish yourself as the expert, you don't own it. Confidence in both yourself and your product is required to win at the sales game. Moreover, knowing how ownership transfers and what role the buyer and vendor play in this context is paramount. We will discuss these important components of your sales presentation in this chapter.

First, here is a little exercise to make sure we are on the same page: a quick quiz (don't hurt yourself, it should be easy since the answers are provided below the question). After the quiz section, we will discuss in detail how each question and answer affects the process of sales ownership and the dynamics of your sales presentation.

Question #1: Who knows the prospect's business better?

Answer: The prospect. If you got this one wrong, you need a sales ego check. No matter what you believe, the prospect will never believe that you know more about their business than they do.

Question #2: Who knows your product best?

Answer: It will always be you (if you don't believe that, then remove yourself from the sales role).

Question #3: Who knows how best to use your product, you or the buyer?

Answer: Trick question, but glad you tried to answer it. It's actually both which is a little more complicated and we will discuss below.

Hopefully you survived that awful experience of a pop quiz, but as you will see, it is important to understand the answers to these three questions. Let's now look closer at each question and answer and why they are important.

Question #1: Who knows the prospect's business better? *Your prospect.*

This is an excellent place to begin this chapter. Getting this question wrong probably puts you in one of two categories: the grumpy old sales guy who has been selling the same thing for years, or the young "up and comer" who can't control his ego. In case you were wondering, neither one is good for your sales health. No matter what you think or believe, you could never convince your buyer you know their business better than they do. You may know how to apply technology, services or whatever else you are selling better, but not *their* company. Understanding this difference is critical. Too many times, sales presenters lock horns with their audience and want to prove to everyone just how much of an expert they are in a particular industry. They believe this effort will serve them well in developing an expert image and winning over their audience. Actually, it has the opposite affect. It stalls relationship development and is condescending to your buyer in two ways.

First, you are a vendor, not one of their peers. Your mission is to establish yourself as a *product expert* in knowing how it can benefit their company. If you try to take the position of both the product and their business expert in the beginning, you derail the entire Stack The Deck model. You skip the critical learning process about their company, establishing your value proposition and aligning what you have to sell to what they need. Use this progression to *win* them over, not *run* them over. Don't crush them with an ego bull dozer and then look back to see if anyone survived. We will go into a lot more detail in this chapter about becoming a product expert, then how to transfer that knowledge to your buyer.

Second, even if you are selling consulting services, you are still not *their* company expert. You must treat them as unique, but with similar traits and requirements to other companies in their industry. If you were a buyer, would you want to listen to a know-it-all who has all the answers before you even ask? If your buyer tunes you out at the beginning, good luck on getting the check at the end.

Question #2: Who knows your product best? *You are the expert.*

You will always enter the presentation as your product's subject matter expert. As the presenter and sales lead, you have to be believable in this role. If not, it will be very difficult for the customer to trust you as the right vendor. Convincing them to buy is a lot more involved than asking for the check at the meeting's conclusion. Remember, they are the ones that are *buying* not *selling* your product. If they knew so much about your product, why would they need you to present anything? Don't miss this fact since you can draw upon it for confidence in your presentation. Regardless of how you feel internally, the external truth is that your audience assumes you to be the expert--so act like it.

> A successful presentation is made up of small wins along the way, not a big finish.

The alternative is giving way to the nerves and spending the rest of the meeting trying to shake off a rocky start. How many times have you attended a presentation and the speaker starts out quiet and nervous, only to open up at the end with an engaging personality once they get comfortable? These initial moments are where you differentiate yourself and start implementing your meeting strategy.

A successful presentation is made up of small wins along the way, not a big finish. If you are too pre-occupied trying to suppress your shaky knees, golden buying signals and opportunities may pass you by. Insecurity can also ruin a presenter by compromising their outer demeanor and interaction with their audience. By not feeling confident with the subject matter or environment, they begin falling apart before they ever step to the front of the room. These inferior feelings also cause a presenter to assume the audience already senses weakness and knows more than they do. I have even seen insecurity go as far as to create an adversarial relationship between the speaker and audience. The presenter in this case was paranoid and believed the attendees were just waiting to hear something to disagree or challenge her on. This defensive attitude was obvious and destroyed any goodwill and audience confidence she could hope to generate. How then does a presenter avoid breaking down and demand the respect of the audience as the product expert? I'm so glad you asked.

I believe that you can extract the best performance from a speaker if they are either talking about something they know or that they believe in.

To better understand what it takes to be the product expert, you first have to disregard what you think of your talents and capabilities. In sales, it doesn't matter what you think of yourself, it only matters what your buyers think of you. To this point, the audience will judge you using two main criterion: technical knowledge and visible emotional. In this context, I use the term "technical" to define broad academic and functional product knowledge. As we will see in the next section, this information is real power in the hands of someone that knows how to use it.

The second criterion, visible emotion is harder to find in sales presenters. Most overlook the importance of connecting with their audience on an emotional level. They feel knowing their product is somehow good enough to win the business. Furthermore, they cannot get comfortable enough with themselves and their subject matter to relax and be themselves. This is why I believe that you can extract the best performance from a speaker talking about something they know or that they believe in. If someone is passionate and knowledgeable about what they are selling, you can expect an engaging performance.

If you want to see this principal in action, talk to a salesperson that is involved in a home based selling or Multi-Level Marketing (MLM) company. MLMs generate billions of dollars every year and are consistently among the fastest growing and revenue generating company types. One of the main reasons for their continued success, and most relevant to this book, is relatively simple. If you attend an at home meeting or party, you will see a display of emotional selling based mostly on personal endorsement and experience. The presentation does not focus solely on just product facts and specifications. The products are important, but the presentation is centered more on the presenter. It is more personal and how these products or services have positively impacted the presenter and others. That is a powerful and very successful value proposition.

Moreover, it is hard for the audience to argue or find fault in someone's personal testimony which creates an instant source of confidence for the presenter. Before they begin their presentation, they already know they are the subject matter expert in talking about themselves. When speaking on a topic or presenting a product that you believe in, it often creates a confidence that is unshakeable. Now combine that with expert product knowledge and you have one dynamic and convincing sales professional.

A great presenter needs to have this type of inherent confidence when talking about their product. There is no secret sauce or short cuts in acquiring these traits. It begins with preparation and having solid product knowledge. If you are not prepared and don't know your product, how can you lead a sales meeting? Moreover, how can you expect to be calm and confident? You set yourself up for failure before you even step into the meeting. Worse, you look foolish in front of your audience and have wasted their time. Don't try to "wing it" on emotion and charisma. These traits can get you through a public speaking engagement with set content like a speech, but they won't get you through a sales presentation. Succeeding in the sales environment demands flexibility and your ability to conquer the unknown. You can't show up to a tank battle with a pistol and expect to be victorious.

Again, this is why Stack The Deck is so critical to your development as a successful *sales* presenter. Your sales meeting is not structured with predetermined content. It is a conversation with constant interaction and variables. You're responses and content are constantly measured and your audience will notice if you don't have confidence in your presentation and delivery skills. Buyers are like hungry sharks, swimming around, patrolling the water. They wait for chum to leak out of your pockets in the form of nerves and weak product knowledge. If they pick up on the fact that you are vulnerable, they will painfully take you apart one limb at a time. Developing indestructible confidence is the one of the main goals of this chapter and a founding principal to Stack The Deck. Shark hunting is a lot more fun than paddling frantically for the shore.

Question #3: Who knows how best to use your product, you or the prospect? *You and your prospect.*

I told you it was a trick question since there are two correct answers. It just depends on where you are at in the presentation in determining which one is right. When you walk through the door for the first time, you are the expert. When you leave and if you have done your job, the prospect will be.

Training your buyer to be a product expert is essential because of what happens while you are conducting this exercise and how it impacts their conversations after you leave. Buyers will always hold internal meetings about you and your product and mull over how you influenced them in the time you had (or didn't). Your success or failure will be repeated over and over in their buying discussions. For this reason, you need to empower as many of your attendees as possible to be experts on your product. Convert them into champions fighting for you to win the business. If you cannot get your audience to become active participants and care about what you have to say during the meeting, you are at a distinct disadvantage when your name comes up after the meeting.

> **You need to empower as many of your attendees as possible to be experts on your product.**

In explaining how to conduct this process, we have to start with defining the word, "expert." The official definition is "someone with a great deal of knowledge about, or skill, training, or experience in, a particular field or activity." Your customer is that skilled and knowledgeable someone that knows how your product best relates to their company. In order for the buyer to adapt your product to their needs, you will need to empower them with two types of product knowledge: **academic** and **application**. You become an expert and own your product by using academic information and your buyer will do the same utilizing application information. We will now explore each of these areas and learn how to train both yourself and your prospect on your product.

Academic product information only relates to what you are selling and you will always be the best person to explain its features, advantages, benefits and highlights. However, simply having the ability to spout off product details when asked is not good enough. There are trained circus animals that can probably meet that criterion. In order to achieve expert status and product ownership, you must have *Adaptive Product Knowledge* (APK). I define this as, "the ability to make product features relevant to the immediate sales opportunity." APK is your central data store of product information used to answer questions, create value and align your product with your buyer. It is used to transform your product from something you are selling into something your prospect needs. APK enables this transformation to take place by molding the product to fit different situations, requirements and value propositions. We have already discussed why it is not a good idea to have the same approach for each prospect.

Remember the NFL example in the introduction? Requirements and dynamics may and probably will change between buyers. However, you can bring the same mastery of product knowledge to each presentation, but use it differently every time. APK will help you navigate sales meetings by quickly adapting to new requirements and answering buyer objections.

To this point, how many times do you get in exchanges with buyers during a meeting where you answer questions with a weak rebuttal? Even if you do survive the answer, are you hoping they choose a different line of follow up questions? If you feel insecure when prospects are firing questions, you are not the aggressor and in no position to control the meeting. If the buyer keeps getting stronger with every question, they will realize they have the upper hand. You want them to own the product, not the meeting. If you have APK, it should be like a constant adrenaline drip in your veins providing you an endless supply of confidence…not arrogance. Nothing will turn a buyer off faster than a presenter that knows more than the rest of the English speaking world. Temper your responses with a hint of calm and humility, but make sure they know you have the answers. Whether it is fielding questions or discussing anything about your product, you should feel there is nothing you can't handle. When you are at the front of the room you must be on the offensive at all times. Treat every objection and question as a chance to prove to everyone *you* are the expert. Your demeanor should produce the same effect as you wearing a sign around your neck that shouts: WARNING: I HAVE APK AND I INTEND TO USE IT. OK, maybe the sign would be a bad idea, but you get the point.

You want them to own the product, not the meeting.

Worse than a sheepish answer is an, "I will have to get back to you" response only to find out later you could have said, "Yes." That equals a lost opportunity to make your closing arguments stronger. Guide the discussion in a direction that best suits your product and to a successful conclusion (we will discuss how to accomplish this later in this chapter). You must be able to gain an advantage using your strengths and your greatest advantage should be your product. The "smoke and mirrors" dot com era is over, so go sell something already.

Quick Note: If your company still uses a corporate name with a color, an abstract food and/or inanimate object to differentiate yourselves, my apologies for the dot.com "smoke and mirrors" comment. Foosball anyone?

This brings us to our third CSF (that stands for Critical Success Factor in case you forgot). Adaptive Product Knowledge is critical to your success as a sales presenter and requires a lot of work on your part to attain it.

Critical Success Factor (CSF) Game Time Decisions

Developing Adaptive Product Knowledge

1. *Study, read and absorb all company manuals and training materials*
2. *Interview individuals responsible for your product's development*
3. *Interview individuals responsible for your product's support*
4. *Research marketing and sales models and any whitepapers that may have been written on your product*
5. *Interview your product's end users and/or customers*
6. *Interview the technology leads (if applicable)*
7. *Research the industry and contact analysts and consulting organizations that may have published research papers*
8. *Look at the historical trends of your industry and interview anyone that may have had your role in the company in the past*

(examples and more resources are available at www.stackitonline.com and the Appendix)

I know that a lot of these points seem extremely obvious, but it is astounding how many people in charge of sales have not completed these entry level tasks. Specifically, **#1: *Study, read and absorb all company manuals and training materials*** is one of the most neglected efforts in our sales culture today. One of the main reasons is that it is probably the most painful of all since it involves old fashioned studying and retention. The longer we are removed from organized study, typically the less motivation we have to research and apply ourselves to this type of effort. We forget the skills needed to successfully retain information and then use it to our advantage. Don't cram! Space out your study sessions into small segments of no more than 45 minutes and don't multi-task while you are focusing on materials. Watching football or sitting poolside with a training manual on your lap doesn't count as applying yourself. Focus and dedication will help in easing the learning curve when you begin this difficult task.

A light literal understanding of your product is superficial and of little value when the pressure is on.

When you are reading materials, make sure you are not just skimming or building facts for your presentation. A light literal understanding of your product is superficial and of little value when the pressure is on. Never be satisfied with a vague idea of your product. You have to dive deeper into the perspective of both buyer and seller. Look intently into product design and intended uses and try to find the association between content and application. Ask yourself questions like: How do these features benefit the intended application? Why was it designed that way? How would a customer adapt this to their business? Constantly challenging the training content and product information will push you past simply being able to recite the product features.

After #1 in the CSF above, most items are straight forward, but you will notice that many contain interview tasks. They are meant to be done *before* you begin presenting to buyers and meeting with prospects. The size of your company is not important. Anyone involved, including the business owners, are critical to this discovery effort. All of the 'interview points" in this CSF are to ensure you understand the people intimately involved with the behind the scenes development and the finished product. For example, you can learn a lot from the customer support personnel since they deal with end users. What a wonderful place to find objections to your product and how best to strategize on dealing with these weaknesses. If you are going to train yourself to be an expert and fully prepare for your presentation, doesn't it make sense to conduct some due diligence on all facets of your product first?

To properly prepare for your interviews, I suggest making a brief questionnaire for you to fill out while you are talking with these groups. You should also include subjective questions that encourage positive feedback. However, be careful not engage employees in a Q & A session that makes them feel like you are collecting sound bytes for their upcoming exit interview.

Another benefit of this research will be a great understanding of how your product works (or doesn't). For this reason, you need to include the customer and/or end user in your research efforts to give you the buyer's perspective. This information will go a long way in helping you better relate to your prospect since they are the specific group you are trying to convince. If you can find a customer that is willing to discuss their sales decision and experience with you, it can lead to priceless insight into what was influential in making their decision. When a buyer tells *why* they bought, that is the modern day equivalent of buried treasure.

I have included an example of two types of questionnaires below: Internal and External. It is important to note that these interviews can take place over the phone or in person. I have had productive conversations in either context. I also recommend that you wait until your product or service has been fully delivered before you begin interviewing any customers. You are searching for solid answers through experience and time doing business with your company. A customer that just completed their purchase is typically not a good candidate except for why they decided to purchase.

These are general questions, but they should provide you with a good start in creating a customized questionnaire. Modify these questions to bring more relevance to your product and efforts as needed.

Internal Questionnaire (when interviewing your company representatives)

---

1. *What is your role(s) within the company?*

2. *How long have you been working in this specific area?*

3. *What are the greatest strengths of our company?*

4. *Can you give me an overview of our product/service?*

5. *What are the important features of our product?*

6. *Who is involved in building and maintaining our product/service?*

7. *What steps do we take to prepare to deliver our product/service?*

8. *How do we make sure our delivery is successful?*

9. *How do we support our customers?*

10. *What do you think are the biggest strengths of our product/service?*

11. *What are the areas we should target for improvement as a company?*

12. What are the areas we should target for product/service improvement?

13. What do you think our customers say about us to others?

14. What company resources and documentation are available for research?

15. Who else do you recommend I speak with in the company?

In this research effort, keep in mind that individuals that deal directly with what you are selling will give you the quickest path to the information you need. Customer service and support personnel, marketing, business development and direct sales are excellent information sources. Meeting with people from within your company demands the most time and attention, but it will pay dividends if you are patient.

In today's sales culture, not everyone is afforded the kind of time necessary to properly conduct these interviews for product training. This brings us to the common dilemma where you have just been hired, but facing immediate pressure to build pipeline and develop opportunities. You are not fully prepared to sell, but that doesn't stop the sales reviews and requests to be updated on your progress. You are expected to forecast and close business yet have no time to prepare. It is this exact scenario that produces so many inept sales reps. As a result, most choose to forego any quality training and spend all of their time trying to show sales activity. If you are entering a new sales role, industry or selling a completely new product, it is unfair but routine for management to throw you into the sales grinder and expect results. So how do you maintain your course to developing into an exceptional sales professional while concurrently developing pipeline? The Stack The Deck formula has two main ingredients: hustle and leverage.

The first **component**, hustle, is obvious. You must put in more hours into your work than you ever thought necessary. In any new situation there is a learning curve. Corporate culture, management styles, reporting, etc. in addition to product information all need to be studied. Hustling and working overtime to train yourself with the Stack The Deck model is the best way to reduce the time needed to get up to speed. Throw out any preconceptions you have on how many hours it should take and the level of effort that should be expended. You do what it takes and commit to this process without compromise. Gear up for less sleep and longer hours.

Second, and most important, is leverage. Look around and utilize every resource available to you to be successful in both training and selling. Leverage *everything* and *everyone* you can, including your peers. I advise new hires to search out the more senior and seasoned veterans on the sales team and ask them to be included in their sales meetings or conference calls. Schedule time with them to discuss best practices and how they successfully close business. When I have found myself in this situation, I have even gone so far as to have them lead *my* sales meetings. I take notes and absorb as much as I can from both them and the buyer. You can learn a tremendous amount of information and preparation strategies by listening to the questions that buyers ask in sales presentations and the responses given. It doesn't take a genius to figure out that if you will be leading sales meetings, you will soon have to answer those same questions. I also recommend reviewing recent proposals from other sales reps and account wins to see how your product is quoted and sold. For example, if you sell industrial machinery, there may be other components such as warranties, support plans, installation and other costs associated with a typical purchase that you need to incorporate into your presentations. Familiarizing yourself with these ancillary components will help you further appreciate and prepare for what is required to make a sale.

Finally, when conducting interviews *within* your company, you must also ascertain strategy and corporate vision in addition to product information. It is just as important to be a company ambassador as it is to be fully knowledgeable about what you are selling. Higher level executives and managers are the best resources to interview for this type of data. They are the ones that make decisions and are routinely asked to present to audiences on the company's strategy and market direction.

Being able to talk to the history of your company and current customers separates you from a typical sales rep simply trying to sell something. Especially for new hires. When the sales lead can not fluently present their founding corporate principles and discuss key customers, it negatively impacts their presenting image and hopes of being viewed as an expert.

Now let's look at the External Questionnaire designed for interviewing customers and anyone associated with your product outside your company.

External Questionnaire (when interviewing your customers)

---

1. *What is your role(s) within your company?*

2. *How long have you been working in this specific area?*

3. *How long have you been working with our product/service?*

4. *In what area do you use our product/service?*

5. *What are the most important features of our product to you?*

6. *Who is involved from your company in maintaining our product/service?*

7. *Can you describe how we delivered our product/service to you?*

8. *How successful was the delivery?*

9. *How do we support you today?*

10. *What do you think are the biggest strengths of our product/service?*

---

11. What are the areas we should target for company improvement?

12. What are the areas we should target for product/service improvement?

13. What kind of reference would you provide if another customer asked about us?

When you are interviewing *customers* in this process, be cautious. You are now on sacred ground talking to an end client that represents revenue to the company. Make sure you consult with whoever is in charge of the customer relationship before you begin so they are aware of what you are doing. Your own sales team represents customers that are already sold. Therefore, they are typically the best individuals to tell you what customers and specially which contacts within that company you should talk to help develop your product knowledge.

However, when you are talking to current clients, put a "customer service" spin on all your discussions and do not put yourself in a position of power. Doing so will create the customer's expectation that you can do something if they raise objections about their current situation. It also will put you at odds with just about anyone that was involved with the sale and/or ongoing support. You have to make sure you get solid answers to questions like why did they buy your product? Who else did they consider and what was attractive about your competition? A quick note on that last question pertaining to selecting other vendors: if your company is failing to deliver the goods, the last thing you want to do is ask your customer about who else they could have chosen. Reminding them they could have

> **You will never be selling something that is 100% perfect, so find out where the holes are so you don't step in them during your next presentation.**

picked a different vendor and add new fuel to their discontent fire will not get you on any Christmas lists.

Your discussions with current customers are key since you can hone in on workflow, business processes and how your product presents advantages and possibly disadvantages to their company. You will never be selling something that is 100% perfect, so find out where the holes are so you don't step in them during your next presentation. It is all about preparation and having all the facts, not just the good ones. If you know both your product's strengths and weaknesses, you can be very effective in controlling how your audience interacts with your presentation and views your product.

If you are the first in your company to read this book, proceed with caution and slowly take each step forward. Keep in mind that conducting this type of research is new ground for most people and if you cause any problems, like upsetting customers, it will derail this important process. You must be introduced by your company's representative for that customer to get in and get out with the right information, from the right person.

This brings us to the second type of product information: **application**. It directly relates to how your prospect will use your product or service. Unlike the data derived from the interviews and research efforts mentioned above, this information is discovered after you arrive *with* your audience. You already are a product expert using Adaptive Product Knowledge. Now you need to guide them through the expert training process using **application** product information. This phase is critical to your success. Why would someone buy anything, if they didn't first fully understand its value and how best to use it?

Every prepared Stack The Deck sales professional will show up armed with Adaptive Product Knowledge. However, one last weapon in your arsenal is needed: a *Product Presence*.

A Product Presence is the combination of Adaptive Product Knowledge and dynamic presentation skills. APK and Product Presence are different in that APK has nothing to do with the audience. It is all about the presenter having complete and flexible academic knowledge of their product. APK is an internal tool whereas a Product Presence is an external presenting weapon. It starts with APK as the platform then evolves into an influential and authoritative presenter persona. It is where the audience begins to see you not only as the subject matter expert, but as the visionary needed to solve their problems. Developing this presence is difficult because it requires you to be fully versed on all aspects of what you are selling. This is why your efforts in collecting your academic product information and developing APK is so critical. You must feel like you have an entire armory of facts, features, statistics and knowledge that you can successfully wield at any moment. Remember, we are talking about how your prospect is going to use your product, not what it does or how it works. A Product Presence is more like the ability to control and/or influence any situation rather than answer questions. This is one of the most critical transitions you can make as a sales presenter and it will always be used while presenting. The moment you achieve this breakthrough with your audience is when *they* know with absolute certainty that you are not just selling, you are the one that will lead them to the Promised Land.

The sequence begins when trust emerges, questions instead of objections are posed and guidance is solicited. This is your chance to begin empowering them with a road map to use *your* product to solve *their* problems. Of course, you are not transferring the actual ownership of your product yet. You are building a vision for the buyer to incorporate your product into their business. Your buyer will always know their business better than you, period. Your job is to foster the discussions and direction of how to apply the product knowledge you have presented. How best to adapt your product into their processes and environment is where the selling begins and presenting ends. Your presentation should take on a completely different dynamic: one of consultation and interview with the overlay of confidence. This is a very exciting time to be the presenter since you can see the fruits of your labor and your preparation pay off. The buyer begins telling you all the reasons why they need and will buy your product. Your job is to listen. Once you see these signs of success, it begins the process of transferring the ownership from you to them and training them to be the expert. It is also the final point of this chapter and will complete our discussion on application product information.

There is no real secret to training your buyer to be the expert during your presentation. A customer training effort is making sure they understand all aspects of your product and how to apply it to their business. You must remember your personal progression through learning about what you are selling and what made that easier for you. Start out with simple product descriptions and general company information. Then move to more specific topics like how it would be used, applied or integrated into their company. (we will outline best practices and techniques at gathering this information later in the book). Your job is to see the entire sales meeting landscape and where you need to take your buyers. Use all of your tools and knowledge to start pushing your value proposition and why they should care about what you have to say. This process should cause a lot of heads to nod in agreement and private dialogue amongst the attendees. This is the first sign you are getting through to them. They will want to make sure they are grasping the presentation content and many times will huddle to discuss.

When they stop talking they will let you know if you have the green light to continue. This may not be a private conversation at all and may be an open exchange between two employees on the buyer side. Do not interrupt these discussions as they are critical in the progression of them becoming experts. Only intervene when they have missed a critical point or are saying something wrong about your product. A minor correction helps, but do not get directly involved. I have been in sales meetings where the presenter believes they know what is being asked then tries to insert themselves into the conversation. This is not the time to try to earn your expert stripes. Don't miss an opportunity for the buyers to come to a positive conclusion or agree that you are on track *on their own*. Again, this is an internal discussion and it is a very positive sign that they are beginning to take ownership and an active role in your presentation. They will begin to discuss how this would apply to their company where you can now assume the role of facilitator. If you can achieve this dynamic during a short presentation, you have done well for yourself.

A word of caution: do not let them control the presentation tempo or fire off random questions. You want them to feel like they are arriving at these conclusions on their own, but not to forget who is getting them there. Most of the time buyers will assume they have the whole story and then just want to get their questions answered to finish off the meeting. Don't let this happen. Hold them to the agreed agenda and answer an out of sequence question with something like, "John, that is a great question and we will address that in a few minutes" or "I have a slide prepared for you specifically on that subject since I thought that would be important to you." You get extra credit if you can say the latter since it shows them you are well prepared. Training your buyer to be an expert on your product requires you to be more like the bumper guards on a pinball machine than the actual flippers striking the ball.

If you have ever seen a pinball machine, you know there are obstacles everywhere and the only place the ball can roll freely from top to bottom is between the flippers you control. Of course, this is the last place you want the ball to go since it will end your turn or perhaps the game. At first glance, a pinball layout looks like mass chaos and your first few balls played on any new machine are reactionary. For the most part, with each strike of the ball, you are discovering the different point values and where the maximum scoring bumpers are located. After you have played a few balls on a particular machine, you can start timing your hits to guide the ball to gain points. You are now controlling the chaos.

What happens after your first few balls played on a new pinball machine should be exactly what happens to you during training your buyer to be an expert. You should be constantly observing everyone and forming your training strategy. Ask yourself, "Who are the decision makers and influencers? Who looks stubborn or easy to convince?" Assessing their personality types will be one of your biggest challenges and will affect the expert training process. Once they have begun their internal discussions as mentioned above, strategically insert comments like, "Good point, David. We did address that change in our latest product version," or "We have now included that in our standard package." Good confirming statements and adding value where necessary will win you points. Interrupting or changing the course of their conversation like saying, "We do have that feature, but we also have another product that relates to that…" or "I don't want to get ahead of ourselves, but we have added some functionality to that…" will lose you points. Remember, buyer training must have a firm, specific progression that is directed by you. Stay on course. You are the product expert and should know the steps needed to become one.

> **If there is doubt, there cannot be a decision to buy.**

It is just as difficult to train yourself with a scattered approach, as it is your buyers. More importantly, you cannot jump around and expect anyone to follow you to the close. If they understand the first feature, then move to the next, and so on. If there is doubt, there cannot be a decision to buy. The buyer is the ball in this game and you control where and when it gets struck and how many points each action is worth. Like the ball, you don't want the buyer leaving the meeting until you have extracted the maximum points possible on your turn. Set the process in motion then drive it home.

I believe many of life's lessons come in the form of experience and the one I share below has evolved into one of my favorite sales principles.

My brother and I found a very large tire in our neighborhood. Too big for a tire swing, we had other ideas on how best to use it. After we rolled it up and down our neighbor's steep driveway for a few "safety tests," we were ready for our first passenger. The only person we knew we could convince was our little sister and after a series of tough negotiations, we loaded her in the tire. I must admit looking down at the incline and the possibility of oncoming traffic, I would not have gotten in. We positioned the tire as before to roll from our neighbor's driveway over to ours. We believed it would be something of a cartoon scene with our sister rolling over again and again laughing and bouncing the whole way down. Good intentions...really.

We then sent her on her way at full speed. However, we never compensated for her hands waiving outside the tire and her screaming every time she bounced. This threw the tire completely off balance and once it began to rotate, it went in a completely awkward direction toward obstacles like landscape rocks, trees and mailboxes. Our crying and hysterical little sister was now tumbling end over end inside a huge tire out of control. She hopped a curb then took out our mailbox at full throttle. That stunt cost us 2 weeks of grounding, our allowance to pay for the mailbox and the promise to never roll our sister down the driveway again.

Think of this story every time you start your prospect down the path of becoming an expert on your product. You have to consider all of the angles and look for hazards and obstacles in advance. Skipping this important step will undoubtedly put you at risk of running off course by blindly pushing and just hoping. Guide them, encourage them and sell them, just don't hit a mailbox.

Chapter 2 Review

---

1. You Are The Product Expert

You will always enter the presentation as the product or service expert. If you do not execute and are not convincing, the customer will not allow you to mold what you have to sell into what they need. Remember, they are the ones that are *buying* not *selling* your product. If they knew so much about your product and advantages, why would they need you to present anything? Draw upon that fact for confidence in your presentation. Regardless of how you feel internally, your audience believes you are the expert--so act like it.

2. The Two Types Of Product Information

Academic *(what your product does)* and **Application** *(how the customer will use it)* are two entirely different information types. The first type involves you beginning and ending as the expert and the second will hopefully end with the prospect filling that role since they know their business the best.

3. Adaptive Product Knowledge (APK)

Adaptive Product Knowledge is the ability to make product features relevant to the immediate sales opportunity. You must be able to mold your product to fit different situations and build a compelling value proposition for every buyer you are trying to sell.

5. Product Presence

A Product Presence is the combination of Adaptive Product Knowledge and dynamic presentation skills. It is where the

---

audience begins to see you not only as the product subject matter expert, but the right person that will be able to assist them in adapting your product to their needs. The moment you achieve this breakthrough with your audience is when they know with absolute certainty that you are not just selling something, but able to solve their problems.

6. Think Pinball

Visualize the sloped surface of a pinball machine moving the ball downward through the bumpers and obstacles. You are in command of everything involved including where and when the ball gets struck. It is difficult to know where the ball is going to end up, but strategically placed bumpers, a declining surface and obstacles guide the ball to the bottom. Set the process in motion and don't go on tilt.

Chapter 3

I'm Going To Hollywood

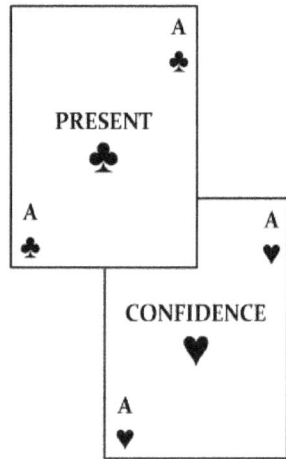

"Win the crowd, and you will win your freedom."
Proximo, from the film <u>Gladiator</u>

Everything we have discussed so far has more to do with preparation structure and your presentation approach. It is no accident that we have covered these topics in this order. First, you must be 100% confident with what you are presenting to be effective. It sounds simple, but too many sales people will work on polishing their delivery and speaking skills and neglect building a sound foundation of product knowledge. You are there to sell your product. Your confidence as a presenter should come from the fact that you know everything about it, not that you can smoothly deliver a sales pitch. Once you can honestly consider yourself an expert, now you can work on your image and winning over your audience.

The secret to developing a great presenting image and succeeding at influencing your audience is found in the glamour and lights of Hollywood. A great movie never goes right from someone's imagination to the screen. The process of producing a movie requires multiple steps. It moves from screenplay to casting then to filming and production. It is a lot of work and demands a master project plan. The script is brought to life by actors making you believe they are those characters. There is always character development and time for the audience to get to know and relate to them. Directors want you to experience chemistry and believe what you are seeing is real throughout the film.

They constantly scrutinize you to determine whether or not you are trustworthy, experienced and knowledgeable.

When you begin to prepare for your presentation, approach it much the same way of watching a finished film and you are the star. Simple questions need to be answered before you arrive. How does your presentation begin and end? What are the plot and personal agendas of all attendees? Are you starting in the right place and using slides that will earn your way to the close?

Conversely, a movie that moves too fast with no time to relate and connect, generally results in poor reviews. Too many times salespeople try to close prematurely and do not gain the confidence of the prospect. Don't forego the same character and story development process with your prospect that Hollywood success is based on. The human element is critical to consider in any sales situation. A cliché rule that is proven time and time again is that people buy from people they like. If they don't connect with you, you won't be visiting the bank anytime soon to make a deposit. Don't miss this fact because it will be your downfall if you believe that all you have to do is deliver a good presentation with a good product. Any arrogance or assumptions made that you already have the business won will eventually cost you the deal or compromise your sales effort during the sales cycle. Buyers look beneath the surface at the person leading the meeting. They constantly scrutinize you to determine whether or not you are trustworthy, experienced and knowledgeable. Those are the traits of a vendor they will buy from.

A great presenter will find common ground with their audience. They will change speaking speeds and either turn up or turn down the level of complexity depending on instant feedback and reactions. This is difficult in a formal presentation format since you are the only one talking and rarely get a steady stream of audience participation. However, there are techniques you can use to connect with your audience. Search for eye contact, people taking notes and body language as your visual clues that you are getting through to them. Adjusting your presenting style to match the room can only begin when you are focused on selling both yourself and your product. If you are still struggling with product knowledge while presenting and it is distracting you from focusing on your audience, you need to re-evaluate your readiness to be the sales lead. Substance and foundation first.

In a more casual sales setting where you are leading a discussion and not formally presenting, ascertaining this information is much easier. You can solicit questions and follow a more relaxed tempo that invites exchanges with your buyer. You can tell by the nature of their questions, posture and attitude how your content is being received. You can also pick up on clues that perhaps your presenting style is either too casual or fast paced. It is possible to pick up a lot of clues by taking the whole interaction between you and your audience into account. Process every word and action first, and then respond to their question. For example, if they pose questions that begin with, "Ok, hold on…" or "Wait a minute…," or put their hand up to gesture "stop", you know you are moving too fast. This causes them to sit up in their seat for short periods of time trying to catch what you are saying. One by one they will fall off and sit back when you lose them if you are running too far ahead.

Conversely, if they are beginning their questions with, "We have seen that before…," or "We are familiar with that, so what else…," you are probably moving too slow. Moving slower causes the audience to get fidgety. Don't let them believe they have time to check their email and write out a shopping list without missing anything. The ability to tailor your presenting style in real time is critical to the success of your presentations. Similar to a movie that accelerates too fast or develops too slow, you run the risk of alienating the people who write the checks.

When you are presenting, keep the phrase in mind, "character development" and continue to ask yourself questions like, "how do I sound? Do I have the right tone and speed? Am I getting confirmation from the audience?" You have to micro-manage yourself during a presentation. Not making these adjustments risks losing the audience, who in this case, have not paid for a ticket yet to see your show. They get the advantage of deciding whether or not to pay once you are finished.

A great way to make sure you are delivering as the sales lead is to have an honest critique from your peers on your presenting abilities. This will give you some great insight into your strengths and weaknesses. Knowing these are key in character development and evolving into a polished presenter. Make sure you do this before you start presenting and then after each presentation if possible. You will be able to track your development and improvement.

There are countless self-help type books on developing and improving your presenting capabilities. I would recommend that you do additional research to adopt a speaking style that best suits your personality. I will not cover those topics and spare you a Ra-Ra session with a, "You can do it" cheer or other fluffy encouragement. I am all for speaker improvement and your presentation needs to be exciting, but sales presentations are different than public speaking.

You are a sales presenter which means you are trying to sell something. You should be focused on every detail that is going to win you the business, not just being dynamic. This book is a comprehensive guide for sales presenting success and meant to quickly arm you with solid fundamentals so you can avoid common presenting and selling pitfalls. So be prepared for your audience and what you can expect from their personality type(s) and feedback. We have now arrived at our next Critical Success Factor.

Critical Success Factor (CSF)   Playing The Game

Character Development Before and During Your Presentation

1. *Firm initial handshake, eye contact (simple, but effective)*

2. *Match their personality type in how you handle their questions and discussions. If they are brief and to the point, be brief and to the point*

3. *Offer personal data points in casual conversation before and during the presentation*

4. *When you make eye contact, really look and see if you are getting through to them*

5. *Monitor your talking speed and take longer breathes than you feel you need*

6. *Don't be afraid of momentary silence and avoid filler words like "um and uh"*

7. *Always talk highly of your team members and be complimentary*

8. *Always use "we" not "I" unless you work for a one employee company and you do all the work*

9. *Know your buyer's work environment, the pressures they are under and their place in the company hierarchy*

10. *Take notes throughout your discussions about each individual*

(examples and more resources are available at www.stackitonline.com and the Appendix)

Again, these points may appear elementary and obvious to you, but under the pressure and scrutiny of presenting, you have to keep it simple. Most of the points above are straightforward, but as usual, some need additional discussion.

Let's first look at **#3**, *"Offer personal data points in casual conversation before and during the presentation."* This is a very good technique to employ since most of the time you have a few minutes when everyone is being introduced and exchanging business cards. If you get the chance to divulge something personal about yourself that doesn't look too contrived, do it. This will begin the process of character development and getting that to work for you before you begin presenting.

Quick Note: Mention something traditional like kids or travel. Stay away from topics like your mother in law or being on probation.

Use all the time before the meeting begins to your advantage. Listen to everything that is going on around you. You should be able to ascertain the mood of the room and some of the personalities you are up against. If no information is available, then you will have to monitor as you go.

#6: *"Don't be afraid of momentary silence and avoid filler words."* If you are not a brick layer, then your success does not depend on filling all the gaps. Silence is good in your presentation, especially if you are trying to make a point. It creates emphasis with dramatic flair and commands attention.

#8: *"Always use "we" not "I..."* One of the most annoying traits of a speaker in my opinion is when they use "I" instead of "we." Did they accomplish all of what they are presenting by themselves? Probably not. Will the buyer only deal with one person for all of their needs? Hopefully not. Besides, an "I" company always looks smaller regardless if one person is all you need to deal with. It also disheartens your attending team members and suggests their presence is not needed at the meeting. Don't alienate your audience with this arrogant attitude and remember it is a team game. You are under constant scrutiny, so don't give your audience any additional ammunition to sink your personality ship.

Reviewing **#9,** *"...know their place in the company hierarchy"* is one of the most critical on the list. Most of the time, your initial contacts are not the end decision makers. Winning over these individuals does not get your product sold. However, they are very valuable in the selling process. They can tell you who is driving the project, writing the checks, what is the decision criterion and even competitive vendor data. Be careful not to be so focused on winning over these initial contacts that you stop looking over their shoulder to see who they report to.

Only when your audience connects with you is when you can push your agenda.

In your continued development as a prepared and polished presenter, character development is crucial. Remember, people buy from people they like. Only when your audience connects with you is when you can push your agenda. You can't create this connection without charisma and personality and unfortunately these are the last traits to be visible to an audience. You have to get past the nerves, environment, and product alignment in order to feel comfortable and be yourself.

Taking control of the variables through sound preparation techniques and product knowledge accelerates this process. There are many distractions to a presenter and you have to set yourself up for success. Only when all stumbling blocks are removed can a presenter engage the audience as themselves. Actors refer to this as getting into character and playing their role. Great performances often generate standing ovations and if you are effective, you can probably expect a warm reception at the bank.

Chapter 3 Review

---

1. Be The Star

When you begin to prepare for your presentation, approach it much the same way of watching a finished film and you are the star. How does your presentation begin and end? You need to provide enough time, information and personality to your audience so they can relate to your experiences and start pickn' up what you are puttin' down.

2. Find Common Ground

You have to change speaking speeds, posture and either turn up or turn down the level of complexity depending on audience feedback and reactions. You must search for eye contact, people taking notes and body language as your visual clues you are getting through. Adjusting your presenting style to match the room can only begin when you are not concerned about anything else, but selling both yourself and your product.

3. Character Development

The ability to tailor your presenting style in real time is critical to the success of your presentations. Continue to ask yourself questions like, "how do I sound? Do I have the right tone and speed? Am I getting confirmation from the audience?" You have to micro-manage yourself during a presentation. Not making these adjustments risks losing the audience, who in this case, have not paid yet for a ticket to see your show.

---

4. Be Yourself

People buy from people they like and only when they begin to connect with you is when you can start reeling them in. Preparation and product knowledge are the prerequisites. Then content, audience and pressure all have to be conquered. As soon as you can master these elements, you can engage the audience as yourself. Charisma and personality are always the last to be visible to an audience. You have to get past the nerves, anticipation of tough questions and other environment factors in order to focus on your product and presenting.

A
♣

PRESENT
♣

A
♣

A
♥

CONFIDENCE
♥

A
♥

Chapter 4

What's For Dinner?

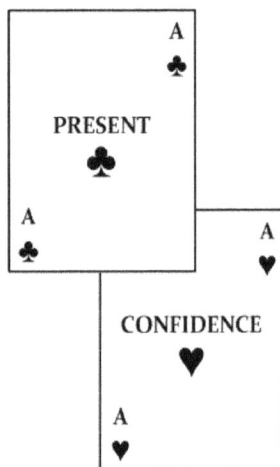

"Always take a good look at what you're about to eat. It's not so important to know what it is, but it's critical to know what it was."

Unknown

You hear of this much anticipated restaurant downtown named the Capricious Café opening on Friday night so you pull some strings to get a reservation. You arrive and are shown to a fantastic corner table with a great view. The server greets you right away and immediately asks you what you would like to order tonight. You politely respond to him that you were not given a menu when you sat down, but he brushes aside your statement with a subtle smile. He tells you that this restaurant is revolutionary in their customer approach. "You do not view a menu here," he says. "You make a suggestion for what you think you would like to eat. Your request is then considered by the head chef and he decides whether or not we can accommodate you." Taken back, but willing to try something new, you suggest a Filet, sautéed spinach and some kind of potato. When you complete your suggestion, the server smiles and then tells you they don't serve steak, but they have some wonderful fish available! How absurd would this style of service and approach be for a restaurant?

The first step in understanding how this restaurant analogy can be used for sales presenting is recognizing that there are two roles played in this example: the server and guest. The server at this restaurant has all of the information while the guest has limited, if any. The guest can only see what has been served on the surrounding tables or what has been discussed before walking in the restaurant. The server on the other hand has all of the necessary data to make the guest's experience a pleasant

Generalizing a presentation feels safe to an ill-equipped presenter that is not confident with their content.

one. He is equipped to host the visit from start to finish while the guest does not have a clue of what to expect. Clearly then, we have the ones with the information and the others who have to ask for it. It should be no mystery to you who has more influence. Information is power.

At our restaurant, a typical salesperson would be a guest. Like showing up without any knowledge of what they can or cannot order, most sales reps arrive at the sales meeting not knowing exactly how they will be selling to their buyer. As a result, most sales presenters construct content and sequence slides based on what's comfortable *for them*. At first glance, this approach makes sense. To make a good first impression, you want to eliminate or reduce variables. Generalizing a presentation feels safe to an ill-equipped presenter that is not confident with their content. Avoiding specifics operates much like an insurance policy. How can the presentation miss the mark if it never takes a shot? Unfortunately, if prepared in this manner, the finished product looks more like your audience having to pull a string to hear you speak. The same content and deck often produces the same sales pitch and demeanor, possibly even the same voice inflections and mannerisms. While consistency is rarely a bad trait, in this context it can be your downfall. The most important group in your sales meeting are the buyers and they will be different every time. Don't be so concerned with insulating yourself against failure that you neglect to include relevant and new slide content. Comfortable for you is potentially missing the mark for your buyer.

To speed up the process of changing decks and customizing on the fly, I suggest indexing. I create sub-folders where I store my customer specific data in "My Documents" if you use Microsoft Windows. I keep a general folder file named "PowerPoints" where the basic decks are saved. This gives me a pool of slides, graphics and content I can cut and paste from if needed. I also have customer specific file folders under the heading "Sales" for individual companies. For example, say for TJC Distributing (see diagram below), I will have a specific deck saved with a date in their folder along with contracts, relevant information, etc. This saves me time if a new deck is needed for a distributing company. I will always consider any of the companies that I have presented to in the past when a new opportunity arises. If I can find a company with similar needs or requirements, I will revise that deck instead of creating a new one. Once completed, I will rename it and save it in the new company's folder. It may sound elementary, but I cannot calculate how much time this approach has saved me. In addition to the time, I arrive with a prospect specific presentation every time filled with familiar content for me to present. This will also eliminate the mindset that since your product hasn't changed, neither should your presentation. The graphic below shows you what my folders look like in My Documents.

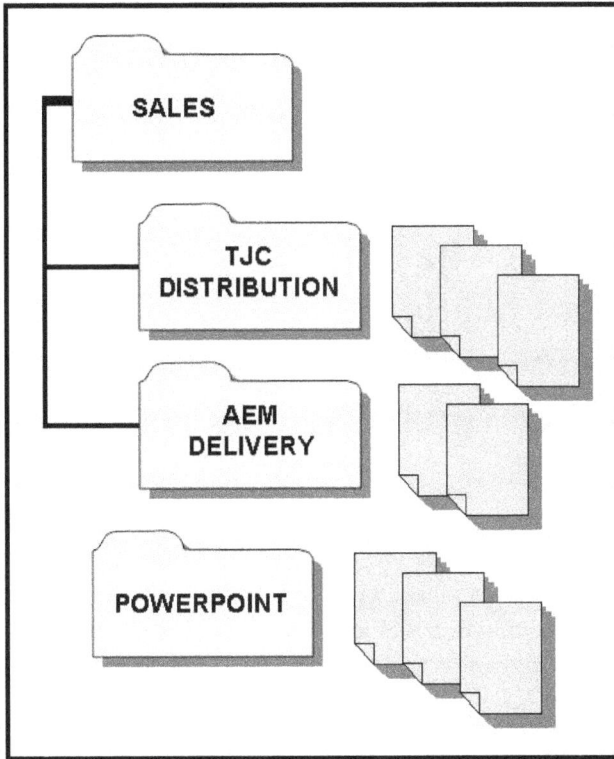

However, there is a monumental difference between using templates and content from the same deck to create new ones and using the same deck every time. Be careful not to fall into a pattern where your changes become less and less and eventually you start using the same deck for everyone.

If you rely on a deck not tailored to your prospect's needs, you are showing up prepared the same way for a different audience each time. Remember our bet at the beginning of this book and stacking the 4 Aces in your 5 cards? You must be equipped with a presentation that allows you to improve your odds and gives you the best chance to win. Your presentation content acts as your supporting cast to help drive you to the close, but it also controls the presentation flow and what is discussed. You need to have a road map in mind of how you are going to get them to the close and spend time on what your prospect needs to hear, not what you want to say. The presentation deck and supporting information you bring with you is going to greatly influence your meetings direction.

> ...The confidence the audience has in you is not nearly as important as the confidence you have in yourself.

So how do we break this cycle and operate with the elite percentage of sales professionals? If we reverse the scenario in our restaurant example and you become the server and not the guest, we have our answer. You, as the server, know what ingredients you have in the kitchen and the head chef's strengths and weaknesses. You also know what dishes have been served already that evening and with what success. The server has the ability to either make or break the experience. As the server in this context, you are prepared to suggest what would be good for your guests to guide their decision. Avoid arriving at a, "No, we don't have that tonight" and instead, discuss what is on the featured menu. You are no longer the guided; you are the guide. This is the role you must play as the sales presenter and the product expert in the room. You have to know where you are going and your audience has to believe and trust in you enough to follow.

However, the confidence the audience has in you is not nearly as important as the confidence you have in yourself. If you are not confident in selling, how can your prospect feel confident in buying? Audiences will connect with a self-assured presenter regardless of meeting type, but being a good public speaker does not make you a good sales person. Through sound sales principles outlined in this book, you can earn their trust by drawing confidence from knowing your product and being prepared. Remember, it cannot be fake bravado or arrogance. It has to be genuine and believable and your audience will know the difference.

To this point, an interesting experiment was conducted by a professor at Michigan State University. He wanted to test the impact of confidence on the connection between a speaker and their audience. On the first day of class, his teaching assistant mentioned he was running late, so she proceeded to go over the semester's syllabus.

As she was discussing the topics, a student became vocally agitated. He loudly proclaimed that the topics were nothing more than common sense and asked why he was wasting his time and money. Boasting that he already knew the content, he began to pack up his belongings and leave the lecture hall. As he walked out, the assistant suggested he teach the class if he thought he knew so much. At first, the student declined, but then changed his mind. He proceeded to the front of the class, dropped his backpack and picked up the chalk. When he began to write and speak with authority, an amazing thing happened: students began taking notes. After a few minutes of dialogue, he confessed to being the professor and not really a student. He asked the class why they started taking notes when they clearly knew he was one of their peers. The universal response was the confidence he displayed in both subject matter and his stated belief that he could relay the message better than anyone else.

Your prospect, like the students in this exercise, have to believe and trust you can apply your product's features, answer questions and draw upon relevant experiences to get them where they need to go. Like a ski instructor on a ski mountain, a scuba instructor in the water, a chef in the kitchen (you get the point), a sales person in a sales meeting is truly in their element. You have to anchor the entire process and establish yourself as the "go to" person in the room. Moreover, the customer has to trust you because if they choose the wrong vendor, they are now at risk. It comes down to assuming the pro-active role, gaining their trust and owning the important information. Be the aggressor in order to influence the outcome in your favor.

Combining all of these elements together is not extremely difficult in preparing for your meeting. You know all about your product, how it relates to your customers, past successes and failures and how to use that information to your advantage. There is no better time than before you arrive at your sales meeting to be considering these facts, construct a value proposition and align everything you have to your audience. Finalizing your content and deciding on meeting strategy is our next Critical Success Factor.

Critical Success Factor (CSF)   Hedging Your Bet

Content and Meeting Strategy

1. *Create the story board before your meeting*

2. *Define goals, success and next steps ahead of time*

3. *Showcase the most relevant features that coincide with your discussions/previous meetings with the prospect*

4. *Sequence your content so that it first tells the story then builds to your conclusion*

5. *Include hidden slides in your deck and/or bring extra information with you to the meeting*

6. *Do not distribute handouts during your presentation*

7. *Each slide should mostly <u>outline</u> content*

8. *Allow time for Question and Answer (Q&A)*

9. *End the meeting on your terms and thank them for their time*

(examples and more resources are available at www.stackitonline.com and the Appendix)

By now you know the routine, it's time to breakdown this CSF. **#1** *"Create the story board before your meeting"* sounds more like it relates to a commercial or movie than a presentation. In fact, your presentation should follow the same creative process. If you have ever watched a behind the scenes special on the making of an animated movie, it is really fascinating. The artists begin with a story "board" and draw out still pictures from start to finish and consider directing and viewing angles along the way. When a finished board is finally approved, the animation begins. Your presentation should be broken out like a story with a beginning, middle and end. Finalize your story before building your deck. This will help you with mental preparation, visualizing presenting and formulating a closing strategy.

To further this thought, how can you possibly get somewhere if you don't know where you are going? This theme has been referenced many times in this book and **#2,** *"Define goals, success and next steps ahead of time"* highlights this point again. Define what success looks like to you and your team before your meeting. Have your next steps already prepared and agree to what you would like to achieve in the meeting. That way, you are not leaving feeling uncertain of whether or not you actually accomplished anything and have a real gauge for success. We will discuss this topic in greater detail in chapter six.

Skipping ahead to **#5,** *"Include hidden slides in your deck and/or bring extra information with you to the meeting,"* can be a huge advantage. Remember my story of the presentation gone bad when we did not have recap information? Avoid awkward silences while you fumble through past decks or marketing materials by bringing a full compliment of support information. Besides presentation slides, extra information can be in the form of magazine articles, white papers, etc. Some of these items may be good reference material, but too cumbersome to review as a group. For example, if you were discussing how your company was written up in a trade magazine, you would never want to read the entire article to your audience. However, showing them the actual magazine is a great prop and may give you some credibility. Same rules apply for your company's latest press release or an award.

Showing your audience this type of information is a great change of pace to constantly staring at a projector screen. Additional presentation slides work in much the same manner. You may never use them, but additional slides may be helpful to make a point or discuss a specific topic. The technique to embed extra slides in your presentation deck is called "hiding slides." It is referenced with that same terminology in Microsoft's PowerPoint. For example, the presenter can have a slide deck with 25 slides, but the audience only sees 20 in presentation mode.

Quick Note: Hiding slides can easily be done by following these steps. (I am making the assumption you have and routinely use PowerPoint. If not, there are tutorials and resources available at www.microsoft.com/powerpoint).

Here are the steps to hiding a slide(s):

1. *Open your presentation file with Microsoft's PowerPoint.*

2. *Click on the "Slide Sorter View" (the icon that has 4 squares) to view all of your slides at once. The icon is at the bottom left of your viewing pane.*

3. *Decide which slides will be hidden from normal view during the slide show or presentation mode (when the screen only shows the slides).*

4. *Right mouse click on the extra slide(s) you don't want to be seen.*

5. *Select "Hide Slide" and the number of the slide will be crossed out.*

6. *If you need the slide during a presentation, escape out of the slide show. Right mouse click on the slide and select "Hide Slide." Note: The icon for the Hide Slide should be highlighted if it is already hidden. This is a little confusing as Microsoft does not say "un-hide slide."*

7. *Return to your presentation by selecting the Slide Show icon at the bottom left or press Shift key and F5 to view your slide in presentation mode.*

While you are pulling up slides, you should fill the time with "I thought you may want some additional information so I prepared a slide" or something to that effect. If you are not using PowerPoint and are bringing printed presentations, I suggest either printing everything together or only printing your core and grouping all of your extra slides in a packet. As referenced in **#6 "Do not distribute handouts during your presentation,"** be careful with printed materials as it is tough to keep your attendees focused when you start handing things out. You have given them your presentation roadmap and most people like to know where they are going. Consequently, they will start flipping through the pages to see content well in advance of your current discussion point. This causes two problems. First, it distracts them from listening to what you are presenting. Secondly, it may cause them to ask questions about your product content out of sequence. We also discussed this situation and some examples at the end of chapter two on how to respond. Thank them for raising the question and let them know you will be answering it shortly.

The most important point in this CSF is **#7 *"Each slide should mostly <u>outline</u> content."*** An experienced presenter will use slides with minimal text, bullet points and graphics. This forces you to talk to the slide and ensures the audience has to listen to you for information. Most presentations are packed with slides with a ton of text in small font. What happens when these types of slides look more like a page from a book? The audience tunes out the speaker and starts to read the text. Worse, they may just tune out all together. Compounding this problem is that most speakers will read the slide to the audience. Is this story time for adults? The ability to use minimal content in your slides requires a compilation of everything we have discussed so far in this book.

Your presentation techniques of winning over the audience, leveraging Adaptive Product Knowledge and having a Product Presence are crucial to pull this off. If you adapt to this style, you are standing in the front of the room with no crutches, no support and still dominating the presentation. When you are rolling and confident with this technique, your audience doesn't have a choice but to believe you have it together.

The last point of ending the meeting on your terms is the final send off of this chapter because we will cover how to build to the close in chapter six. Do not allow the buyer to dictate how the meeting begins or ends. You established an agenda beforehand, identified what was going to be discussed and hosted the party. Now bring the meeting to a close.

When the meeting adjourns recap your next steps and thank them for their time. High ranking executives like to be appreciated. Acknowledging their time spent with you goes a long way in leaving them with a good impression. If you can guide and control your meeting, like a great dining experience you can count on repeat customers.

Chapter 4 Review

1. Information Is Power

There are two distinct groups in a sales meeting: those with the information and the others who have to ask for it. It is not difficult to figure out who has more power and influence. The goal then is to leverage the information you do have with a well timed buyer Q & A to extract the information you don't. This will give you a complete view of the buyer landscape which is required in figuring out how to close the sale.

2. Take The Lead

You are not the guided, you are the guide. As the sales presenter and the product expert in the room, you have to know where you are going. More importantly, your audience has to believe and trust you enough to follow. It comes down to assuming the pro-active role, gaining their trust and owning the important information. Use it to be the influencer and determine the outcome.

3. Define Success And The Next Steps Prior To The Meeting

Defining success and determining optimal next steps beforehand helps you focus on what you would like to achieve in the meeting. You will avoid the recap discussions on the way back to the airport convincing yourselves it was worth the travel expense and wondering if you accomplished anything.

4. Don't Let Your Presentation Hold You Back

Your presentation has to reinforce your "prospect first" approach. It should enable you to align your product with what you are hearing in terms of needs, objections, etc. You cannot do this if all of your slides are weighed down with text and you simply are hosting story time. The ability to use minimal content in your slides, yet give a complete presentation, requires mastering everything we have discussed so far in this book.

Chapter 4 Bonus Section: *Presentation Tips For Designing Your Slide Deck*

How many times have you attended a presentation and the slide deck the presenter was using was unsightly or unprofessional? It was probably riddled with too many bullet points and endless paragraphs or clip art that made it look like a third grade art project. The slide deck you decide to use is representative of your company, product and you. After all, you are the sales lead and responsible for all materials that are used during your presentation. If you did not approve of the deck, then you should have changed it to better suit your audience and meeting.

Part of chapter four was devoted to discussing how to build the right kind of sales presentation deck. Now we need to discuss how to properly design it to ensure that effort will be worthwhile.

Dr. Keri Stephens Ph.D., Assistant Professor at the University of Texas has researched organizational technology use and taught sales communication courses. She advises that, "PowerPoint should be a visual aid instead of just a bunch of projected text." I have summarized her recommendations for the following key areas:

1. Backgrounds and templates

   Use high contrast color schemes and stay away from gradient templates. A gradient is an effect where color transitions to a different shade or color all together. They tend to drown out any pictures or text that you use when projected on screen. Don't trust your PC screen since it is high resolution and the screen will look different using a projector. Furthermore, using lighter color backgrounds are more forgiving and quite often keep you from having to dim the room lights.

2. Font guidelines

Select your font *color* based on achieving the best contrast to your background. The font *size* rule is easy to follow, the bigger the better. Your slides may look good when you are looking at them on a small screen, but when your deck is displayed on a large screen, you will want large font and less content. The font *type* depends on what is the easiest to read for your audience. Here is a short list of good and poor fonts:

GOOD

- Arial
- Arial Black
- Futura
- Tahoma
- San Serif

POOR

- Serif
- Times New Roman
- New York
- Courier

3. Bullets points: use up to six

Your audience will not be able to follow you and properly retain all of the information you are giving them if you exceed six bullet points per slide.

4. 25 words or less per slide

    f you have any more than 25 words on a slide, there is no way you are going to be able to get through it without dictating a portion of it to your audience. You never want to appear bound to or reliant on a slide deck. Reading word for word is not acceptable. Furthermore, paragraphs of text will distract your audience and they will probably stop listening and try to read as much as they can before you flip to the next slide.

5. Your images are key

    You are no longer in middle school, so your appreciation for hot wheels and finger paints should have dissipated by now. Lose the sound effects and animation as well as the clip art. It is juvenile at best and will detract from the expert presenting image you are trying to establish. Instead, use professional graphics and images that better represent your product and company. There are multiple sites on the Internet where you can find acceptable artwork. A good starting point is searching for "clip art, graphics and/or professional photos."

Chapter 5

Mission Control

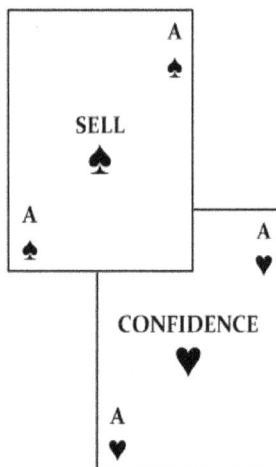

"This mission is too important for me to allow you to jeopardize it."

> HAL 9000 (Douglas Rain) from the film 2001: A Space Odyssey

Almost every movie I have seen about space exploration involves the relationship between the space crew and the team on the ground: Mission Control. They are the team of people in a huge room with monitors and work stations on earth, managing everything from the spacecraft's location to the astronaut's vital signs.

A salesperson's responsibility in a presentation is a lot like running Mission Control. Your job is to facilitate the entire meeting from start to finish. Like building a great story as we discussed in Chapter 4, how does each meeting start and end? You always see sales meetings begin with the basic introductions and then the same sequence of events unroll almost on queue. Think about your last sales presentation. Let me guess, it probably kicked off when everyone sat down and introduced themselves. Then the sales lead looked at the buyer and asked "Well, should we get started?" The attendees nodded, sat down with their cups of coffee and then he opened with, "Our company was founded in 1985 with the vision of...." and finishes off a well structured and canned presentation with "Any questions?" This is an informative, organized and completely clueless way to manage a sales meeting.

Your job is to facilitate the entire meeting from start to finish.

Most buyers assume you are there to present what you have and they are there to listen. Completely false. They are there to tell you why they need your product and it is your job to extract that information before you start presenting. In order for you to be effective, you need the buyer to go first and we will discuss why in this chapter. However, the buyer is going to try to avoid giving you this information up front thus beginning the cat and mouse game of who goes first. Unfortunately, most vendors give in and assume the role of the traditional sales guy with a tired sales pitch. Why? Because they have not established themselves in second position on the pre-meeting call with their attendees and/or they lack the confidence to take a stand and control the initial meeting moments.

Compounding the problem, the buyer already assumes home field advantage and puts the vendor in the position as the *guest* (remember, you don't want to be the guest).

Most buyers feel this tactic forces you into an "objective" presentation handicapping your ability to strategically shape your product to what they need. They can then make their own determination as to your products relevance and value to them. To the contrary, the fact is that this process really does benefit the buyer and not just give you an advantage. If they really need to solve a problem or are looking to improve operations with your product, the best way to do that is to openly discuss issues with you first. The buyer first agenda ensures that the audience will receive the maximum benefit from your presentation.

In the traditional presentation example above, the vendor always goes first and presents what they have to offer. Preceded with some pleasantries, buyers ask an iteration of the famous question: "What do you have for us today?" Then the sales team takes that as their signal to get started and the audience sits back as they let the air out of their presentation balloon. They watch it fly around and around until it runs out of air and falls to the floor never following a consistent flight path. Then everyone plays Q & A with each other and the presentation is used only for reference and graphical support. Does this sound familiar? It should, because it is the way 95% of all sales people run their meetings and presentations.

Salespeople do not push back hard enough on the attendees in the beginning stages of a presentation to obtain what they need first, then discuss their product or service. This is an important point since you may be able to solve some specific pain points or fix a problem with your product while you are presenting. For example, let's give you the job of selling kid's athletic apparel to a large local retailer. You know through your research ahead of time this retailer only offers 2 out of the top 5 competing brands in their kid's department. You are manufacturer #3 in the market and recognize a huge opportunity to gain distribution and drive top line revenue. You want this account because it is located in a relatively weak region for sales in your company. You also know that athletic apparel is a strong category for this retailer's number one competitor a few miles away and is a source of angst among this buying committee. Your retail buyer only has average sales in this category so you ask if they have been conducting well-timed promotions to coincide with local sports leagues. They say they stock plenty of related seasonal shirts and shorts in advance, but do not feature any specific athletic shorts during individual sports leagues. Use this information to your advantage. During your presentation discuss the increase in sales your last customer realized after running well timed promotions featuring your company's soccer and basketball shorts at the start of each respective season.

The better strategy is to build in value, before you start discussing price.

Rather than spend time trying to sell everything, allocate more time selling what is needed. Still offer information and include your other products, just place more emphasis on the opportunity you have identified with your buyer beforehand and during your initial meeting discussions. Adjust your content and presentation using the information your buyer has divulged in addition to what you brought to solve a problem and/or build a vision. Additionally, information such as what might have changed since your last communication, recent mergers or department events might certainly influence your presentation. Ask questions and talk with your buyer *before* you present, then take your place at the front of the room.

Remember the restaurant analogy in chapter three? Information is power. Before you take your shot, you must own that power and transform it into influence. These forces are present and constantly moving throughout a sales meeting. It often shifts between the buyer and vendor very much like momentum in a sports game. Successfully retaining influence is all about guiding the meeting. If the buyer has control, you must wait for your chance to seize it back. To ensure you do not surrender influence up front, establish yourself as the interviewer, not the interviewee. If you are answering questions instead of asking them, you are at risk of veering off course. Moreover, the buyer can manipulate their follow up questions and fire away in any direction. This reduces your value to that of a live commercial that they can shut off at anytime.

Power in a sales meeting is taken, not given. You must earn it and put yourself in position to use it to your advantage. What I mean by earning power is that before you ever arrive for your meeting you should be preparing for everything. Only through sound preparation can you excel through the variables, objections and unknowns in a sales meeting. We addressed preparation in chapter 1 and recall the NFL playbook example. This is where preparation meets execution in knowing your product, having confidence and following a pre-determined, flexible meeting strategy. Like head coaches adjusting their game plan in real time, you must do the same. NFL teams do not create full plans on the sidelines, they have game scenarios already in mind in case certain events take place. They have empowered themselves to make quick decisions to keep momentum (influence) on their side. I encourage you to make sure you have done your homework on preparation. It extends far beyond just knowing your product and meeting agenda. Preparation is not only used in sound presenting methods, but it is crucial in shifting the balance of power.

Power in a sales meeting is taken, not given.

In order to successfully retain power in a presentation, you must maintain a patient, professional exterior, while underneath you are processing a thousand bits of information. Calculate who has what opinion and influence in the group. Filter comments and questions being raised by your audience and how you are going to address them in your presentation. Ask leading questions, all within a grand design where *their* answers will lead them to selecting *your* product.

For example, suppose you are selling lawn maintenance services and you know that your competition is unorganized and does not clean up after completing their work. They periodically show up late and are not the cheapest company in town. However, they have been around a long time and have a lot of clients. You want to try to win their customers over, but you don't have a lot of time to convince your prospects in door-to-door sales. Which is a better opening question, "How much do you currently pay for your lawn service? (knowing you are cheaper)" or "Does the service that you have now arrive on time and sweep and bag to your satisfaction?" Sure it would be easy to lead with price and simply try to beat the other company out. At the same time, how easy would it be then for the home owner to go back and leverage your new price to get a better one from their current provider?

I know this is a simple example, but it represents a simple principle that is consistently missed in sales meetings. The better strategy is to build in value, before you start discussing price. Try to influence your buyer's decision criterion to something that will be hard for your competition to match. Most savvy buyers are going to research who else has what they need anyway. Why not make it more difficult for them to find a better fit than you?

There is a popular corporate question that asks, "What is needed to make a better leader, authority or influence?" The answer in my opinion is influence. It takes a lot more skill to

shape and suggest than to simply order someone to go in a particular direction. Especially if they feel they arrived at a particular decision on their own. You will find countless books on having the "power of influence" on people and I recommend that you do some reading on the subject.

In this context, influence is used to guide the prospect to a conclusion of buying your product. This is achieved through the power to suggest, control and navigate your way to the close which is an invaluable asset.

Knowing how to influence your presentation outcome through timing, preparation, power and control is our next Critical Success Factor.

Critical Success Factor (CSF) The Odds On Favorite

Presentation Influence

1. *Manage the initial moments of the presentation*

2. *Interview the buyer first*

3. *Listen carefully and take thorough notes*

4. *Collect the names of people that made comments and attach that data to their name in your notes*

5. *When they tell you the reasons why they will and won't buy, write them down*

(examples and more resources are available at www.stackitonline.com and the Appendix)

#1 *"Manage the initial moments of the presentation"* and #2 *"Interview the buyer first."* If you have followed your checklists and Critical Success Factors from previous chapters, you will have already established that you need the buyer to go first. You can reinforce this by listing it specifically on your agenda. If you recall, you will conduct a pre-meeting conference call to discuss what will be covered as referenced in chapter one. This is where you request that they open the meeting with giving a summary of what they need and some history on their company. It is crucial to the success of your sales presentation that you extract as much information from your attendees before you have the floor. Have the confidence to hold the line when the meeting starts. Make sure you do not get run over by your attendees forcing the "vendor first" agenda.

Even if you did not establish yourself in second position during pre-meeting communications, there is still hope. You can use comments like, "For the benefit of my team members that were not involved before this meeting, please give us a quick recap of what you are looking for." If they insist on you going first and it is getting uncomfortable, here is a good compromise. Begin your presentation with a recap discussion and then work in your questions periodically throughout the early portion of your presentation. Confirm the points of interest, objections and questions in a summary format and treat it as part of your introduction. This way you can create dialogue that fits your purpose. You may not get all the information you were looking for, but it's a better start than the alternative. Regardless of how it takes place, you have to conduct your buyer interview or Q & A session first before you start talking about your product.

You must follow an organized path with your questions so you don't lose focus or end up at a dead end.

Keep in mind you cannot just start hurling questions over the table as it defeats the purpose of winning over your audience. If you launch into a hundred random questions up front, the buyer could get defensive. They may consider it too much work to participate since they won't see how watching you aimlessly try to extract information is going to help them. More specifically, it is hard for the buyer to justify disclosing that much information without being convinced it is going to good use. Everyone is busy these days and the saying "time is money" is more relevant than ever.

If you have not established enough credibility early in the presentation and your first few questions make you look clueless, good luck on getting them engaged. This is an important point that should not be missed. If the buyer does not feel you can use this data to solve their problem, they will not truly open up. Worse, if they have a negative first impression, their answers will be short with no additional information. If you appear to be flailing around fishing for clues, you will reinforce their defensiveness. This will cause them to push for you to start presenting and just want to listen.

However, if you are organized in your pre-meeting calls and communications, and then your interview, the buyer will perceive value in participating. In their mind, it may uncover the right solution for them and it feels like a healthy exercise to all. You must follow an organized path with your questions so you don't lose focus or end up at a dead end. Think of yourself as a trial attorney gathering evidence through depositions so you can use that information during the trial. This exchange normally takes place at the beginning of the meeting, making it very difficult to establish yourself as the expert. Add this to the list of why pre-meeting interaction is critical to your presentation success. Give your buyer as much information about you ahead of time and always assume they are sizing you up. If they respect you before the meeting, it will make your job easier when you get there. You have to win the credibility battle first. Then you can focus on extracting the data you need in order to give a perfectly aligned buyer presentation.

To illustrate how this process works, imagine I am selling inventory management software to an office furniture manufacturer. When we sit down in the meeting, one of my first questions is going to be business process related and how they currently conduct operations. I know that customer improvement in this area is a core strength of my product. Their answer will be helpful in aligning my product to solve any problems we uncover. My strategy is to start with one item like an office desk that they produce and track how that product flows through their entire supply chain. Along the way I will be looking for inefficiencies, redundant tasks and areas that my software can help solve some issues. As mentioned above, I will not be discussing my product whatsoever at this stage in the presentation. Doing so will throw the Q & A session off track and cause the buyer to become impatient waiting to hear about what I have to say.

Being patient is difficult, but stay focused on the buyer throughout your Q &A. I will then follow up the process dialogue with perhaps some specific competitor and existing technology questions. I do not want to get to the end of my presentation only to find out we are not compatible. If that was the case, I could have spent my time with them either brainstorming on how we could integrate through alternative means or focus on our other products/services that may be a better fit.

Again, the first part of the meeting must showcase the buyer and not the vendor. Maintaining a confident and controlled persona at the beginning establishes you as the product expert. We have thoroughly covered this topic and those first two Critical Success Factor points are the most important in managing your meeting.

In the beginning of the meeting, buyers should be talking more than sellers, period.

#3, "*Listen carefully and take thorough notes..,*" references what you have heard a thousand times. You must listen to learn and you can't listen if your lips are moving. Unfortunately, listening can be challenging for many people, salespeople in particular. In the beginning of the meeting, buyers should be talking more than sellers, period. How can you possibly know anything about their business if you aren't asking questions and listening?

Shannon Cassidy, Executive Coach, at bridge between, inc. says sales presenters should begin with "what" or "how" type questions that will spark dialogue. "Take time to prepare the types of open ended questions you want to ask. Once you ask the powerful questions – W.A.I.T. for the answer. Too often we ask a powerful question and then answer it! W.A.I.T. stands for Why Am I Talking? If you have a good answer to that question – go ahead and speak. If not, be patient and wait for the answer."

Use the 80/20 rule on yourself and/or team at the start of the presentation where 80% of the content is supplied by the buyer. Some sales presenters have committed to this process in planning, but they fail in execution. Every time a buyer raises a point or makes a statement about a need, the sales lead jumps in and says, "We just started offering that feature" or "our customers really like that we do that." You are not selling at the beginning, so zip it. The buyer is talking and you should be taking notes asking open ended and leading questions. Listening to the customer does not include you inserting an advertisement every time you see an opportunity to align your product with the discussion. Your time will come, but your current role is more like a sales therapist coaxing out the pain points and how you may be able to cure them. Once you have all the information you need, or at least what the buyer is willing to disclose, then you start the process of putting it all together for a proper diagnosis and cure.

The last Critical Success Factor point **#6: "..the buyer will always tell you why they <u>will</u> and <u>won't</u> buy."** Listen for the points, number and write them down. When I am taking notes, I organize each page and track who is raising objections and asking questions. I also write down phrases like, "We really don't have that figured out" or, "That is our biggest issue." Pay close attention to what is said because the current discussion topics will soon be buying points and/or objections coming your way. They will resurface and it is your job as the sales lead to be prepared. Attach the names along side the statement and keep a tally of "for" and "against" so you know where you stand at any point in the meeting. You can also use it for a meeting recap, establishing next steps and in your attempt for a firm close if possible. In any sales situation, good note taking techniques will pay dividends for you in your follow up efforts and working your way to the close.

When used individually, these principles will positively impact your sales results. Using them in concert will transform the way you present and sell. These techniques not only apply to the sales meeting, but the entire sales environment around you. Sales opportunities do not just take place in board rooms, but anytime you are discussing your product with someone intrigued enough to listen.

Chapter 5 Review

---

1. First Is Not The Best

Giving a full presentation first forces the process of constructing relevance with the customer to take place after your presentation. You do not have a chance to strategically align your product with their needs and solve some specific pain points while you have the floor. Don't go first.

2. Interview The Buyer...The Right Way

You must follow an organized path with your questions so you don't lose focus or end up at a dead end. Think of yourself as a trial attorney gathering evidence through depositions so you can use that information during the trial. Before you start asking questions, consider the exact data you need to hear in order to give a perfectly aligned buyer presentation. Conducting a structured interview will also give you credibility with the buyer.

3. Apply What You Have Learned

After the Q & A with the buyer is finished, it is now time to incorporate that information into your presentation. Still offer information and include your other products, just place more emphasis on the opportunities you have identified with your buyer. It looks impressive and proves the Q & A session was valuable.

4. Power Is Influence

Real power in a sales context is more like influence through the ability to suggest, control and navigate your way to the close.

Influence is present throughout a sales meeting and often shifts between the buyer and vendor, very much like momentum in a sports game. Keep it on your side since you need it to win over your audience.

5. Are You Listening Or Talking?

In the beginning of the meeting, buyers should be talking more than sellers. The buyer is talking and you should be taking notes, asking open-ended and leading questions. Finally, listening to the customer does not include you inserting an advertisement every time you see an opportunity to align your product with the discussion. Be patient and wait your turn because you will get your chance to present.

Chapter 5 Bonus Section: *Presenting via Web Conferencing*

Wireless email and the emergence of the virtual office have changed the corporate employment landscape forever. New technology has enabled more employees to operate apart from their corporate headquarters, working from home or on the road. As this trend has grown, it has also impacted the way sales organizations manage their team and opportunities. Companies are now encouraging and often requiring that sales development activities be done remotely. Once a prospect is qualified, then a face to face meeting is scheduled.

Web Conferencing providers like NetMeeting, WebEx and GoToMeeting enable a sales presenter to "share" a presentation and/or their desktop view with a group of people over the Internet. Coupled with a conference call, it is a virtual meeting and a very common way for buyers and vendors to interact online. Unfortunately, this new technology quickly exposes sales presenting flaws including lack of preparation, charisma and the ability to manage a presentation. Hosting a Web conference and actually using it to sell someone is something that most presenters have not figured out how to do.

Quick Note: In this section, I am making the assumption that you do not have access to video conferencing. Web conferencing without video is an entirely different presenting environment. Web and video together follow the traditional presenting rules.

Before we dive into a Stack The Strategy for this type of presentation, I need to first remind you that all principles in this book apply in order to give a successful Web conference. Nothing changes in terms of preparation, checklists, etc., except that the vendor does not present in person to the buyer. Be cognizant of this fact as it is tempting to slack on your preparation efforts since you do not have to be face to face with your audience.

Like traditional presenting, preparation for a Web conference is one of the most important efforts you can make to increase your chance of success. Of course, the main difference is that your audience cannot see you. This amplifies awkward silences or any error made in not having the right information on hand. The sound of a presenter fumbling over papers or trying to find a slide in a different deck is devastating to their presenting image. Additionally, all bodily noises such as coughing, sniffling, sneezing or clearing your throat are both distracting and equally as detrimental.

You need to be discussing what you have to offer, not sounding like a professor. This is an area where most presenters fail to have a conversation with their audience. Acknowledge and prepare for this potential pitfall before you host a Web conference. Know that while you cannot be there in person, you can be personal. This disarms a lot of groups when you talk *with them*, not *to them*. Your voice is the only personal attribute the buyer can use to decide whether or not they like you. Presenters often neglect voice inflections or worse, sound nervous or overbearing. The reason this is so damaging, is that most of the time you are on a speakerphone with multiple attendees listening on the other side. Even if the buyers have joined from different locations, it still creates what I call the "Pack Effect." If you sound weak or nervous, your buyers can turn into a pack of wolves devouring a piece of meat with everyone wanting to get in on the action. They do not have to be accountable to a real person, only a voice. If you are arrogantly throwing your weight around on the call as the "expert" and have not earned that title as we have discussed in this book, you will create the same response. They will band together and try to stump you with pointless questions or find holes in your story.

STACK the DECK

If you prepare for the Pack Effect on a Web conference, you can avoid its negative effects and use it to your advantage. Realize they are all on a call together with their peers and perhaps superiors in the company. They do not want to risk sounding ignorant or arrogant either. Do not give them an invitation to sound intelligent at your expense. Using "absolute" statements including words like "never" or "only" will invite a confrontation from those wanting to grand stand and grab the spotlight from you. If you can defend your position after making these statements, then by all means fire away. If not, stay with your value proposition and don't get adventurous. More than ever, you must know where every discussion path leads. If you get lost on a Web conference, you cannot look to your audience for reassurance that you successfully pulled out of a tailspin. You will never know if you truly brought everyone back if you veered off course.

Aside from being prepared, avoid debating individuals one on one in a Web conference. Even if you win on the call, you will lose afterwards. You only have a short time on the phone, but the person you just bested has unlimited access to the rest of the audience to plead their case and convince them you were wrong. You also just gained an enemy in the buyer's camp, congratulations. Instead, suggest an "offline" discussion with the individual. This is a great technique for several reasons. First, it removes risk for both parties since everyone will be listening to your exchange. Second, it shows you are in control and sympathetic to the entire group if it is a specific question that may not interest everyone. Finally, it gives you an opportunity for a one on one conversation where you may be able to extract some additional information in a more private context.

The most important point to remember about Web conferencing is you must be excited about what you are presenting. If you want to find a perfect example of the average Web conferencing presenter, watch the movie, *Ferris Bueller's Day Off.* The actor, Ben Stein, is calling student names for roll call in the most boring, mechanical and lethargic voice possible. Avoid sounding monotone and rehearsed or even more annoying, reading from index cards.

Lastly, your individual attendees may not be in the same room, so they have no accountability for their appearance or activities during the Web conference. If you are not exciting to listen to, they will tune out much faster on a Web conference since you cannot see them. For example, they can mute their desk phone and field cell phone calls, email while you are presenting or worse, talk about you while you are talking to them. I am pretty confident that just about everyone has muted a conference call phone and discussed the presenter at some point in their corporate history.

Clearly, you are a lot more vulnerable on a Web conference and have little control over your audience. Be convincing, be personal, but most of all be yourself since your personality is your greatest asset in a Web conference presentation.

Chapter 6

Working On The Line

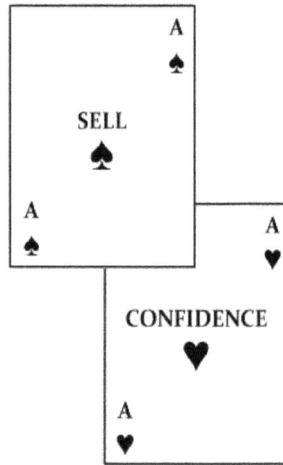

"He who controls the present, controls the past. He who controls the past, controls the future."

George Orwell

In 1907, Henry Ford announced his goal for the Ford Motor Company: to create "a motor car for the great multitude." This was definitely a radical statement, considering the early automobile was expensive, custom-made and reserved for the wealthy.

Henry Ford's initial steps toward achieving his goal were to limit choices including color and move more toward a standard product. The Model T, first produced in 1908, kept the same design until the last one that was produced in 1927. Even though the early versions of the Model T were less expensive than other cars, it was still not attainable for the "multitude." Ford and his team needed to reduce production costs even lower in order to find the right price point. They searched for answers across multiple industries and found if they used interchangeable parts and divided tasks into a continuous flowing process, it would reduce wasted effort and ultimately, cost.

Ford put these principles into a plan and then in 1913, introduced the first moving assembly line ever used for large-scale manufacturing. Ford produced cars at a record-breaking rate and concurrently lowered the price thus achieving his goal of an automobile for the multitudes.

Just because they enjoyed your presentation, doesn't mean they are going to buy from you.

In much the same way that Henry Ford produced Model Ts from an assembly line, your build up to the close should follow the same progression. The finished product from an assembly line is determined by the parts and process used along the way. Likewise, your tactics before, during and after your presentation will determine how successful you are in winning. The close is much more than just managing the final minutes of a sales meeting. A successful approach involves planning, process and strategy.

You cannot simply rely on emotion and "sales savvy" in trying to persuade someone to give you their business. You may be convincing, but <u>winning someone over</u> and <u>winning the sale</u> are two entirely different efforts. How many times has your audience enjoyed your presentation, thought you were likeable and confident, but you didn't get the account? Just because they enjoyed your presentation, doesn't mean they are going to buy from you. The majority of sales presenters accept this routine of winning people over and losing business.

Too many sales presenters attempt to "wing it" at the end of their meeting, relying on good feedback and audience affirmation to carry them to the close. They use too much emotion and not enough mechanics. Keep in mind that when you leave the meeting, all positive energy will dissipate and the buyer is going to base their decision on whatever concrete data points you provided. For this reason, you must train your buyer to be an expert on your product and align it successfully with their needs. Either make a strong case as to why you should win or you will be dismissed as a good presenter with an average product. Leaving the decision up to the buyer is never a good idea. It will force your prospect to make up their own mind about the value of your product and its relevance to them. A structured approach every time will ensure that you hit all of your critical points. You cannot leave the meeting wishing you had said something more or forgetting to address an issue that was raised. These avoidable mistakes will leave the opportunity open for someone else to claim.

To further clarify this point, if you ask a sales rep to define how they regularly close their meetings, you will get a different answer every time. Most presenters have a *pattern* and not a *process* that guides their closing actions and decisions. How can you produce a consistent result without any structure? Remember the pre-shot routine example and constructing a Risk Assessment in chapter one? Those same principles apply to a sound closing strategy. <u>You</u> are the constant element in all of your sales presentations regardless of customer and location. Everything else will change and anything that cannot be defined and planned for ahead of time is a variable.

By now I hope you realize that controlling and identifying as many presenting variables as possible is in your best interest. They include project plans, legal agreements, delivery timelines, etc. In order to receive the actual purchase order or contract, these items need to be dealt with during the sales process. They play a role in closing the sale, but not getting the buyer to say, "Yes." They are merely academic items and have little to do with a buyer's decision to do business with you in regards to selecting the best vendor. When was the last time you were involved in a sales cycle and the decision was based on who had the better contract terms? It happens, but not enough to base all of your sales focus on getting the structure of the deal in place before you have convinced your buyer you are the right choice. Too often, presenters are preoccupied with agreements and project and delivery plans then miss the most important step: convincing the buyer. This may be due to the common "results oriented" sales management where if there is no paperwork, there is no deal. No argument here, just make sure you have your priorities straight going into the last rounds of the fight. Don't get ahead of yourself in the sales process. Win the business first, then worry about getting the paperwork and processes done.

The customer's decision to buy is made long before you ask for them for the order.

If typical sales presenters aren't relying on emotion to close or distracted with paperwork, they are trying to keep score with their competition. They are fixated on finding out which competitors are pursuing the same account. Instead of building a case as to why the buyer should choose them, they waste time interrogating their audience to find out who else is involved and at what price. Typically, this barrage of questions is hurled at the buyer at the end of the presentation. The precious final moments of the meeting are spent trying to accumulate as much information as possible about the other vendors instead of convincing them they are the right choice. I am not suggesting that you don't find out who your competition is in every account. Quite the contrary, but don't do it at the end of the meeting when you should be hammering home your value to the buyer.

Moreover, you look desperate searching for an advantage and relying on your buyer for information at the end you should already have already extracted at the beginning. Let me be clear, it is important to try to find out as much as you can about your competition, but it should be done long before you are trying to close. This information should be covered during your Q & A session so you can outsell your competition during your presentation. I will insert questions that appear inquisitive, but are meant to extract the competitive data I need. For example, "Have you looked at these kinds of products before?" or "Have you talked with anyone else regarding these issues and do you think you can find a solution?" The second question is critical and should always be asked for two reasons. First, it allows you to assess how optimistic they are that a solution exists and second, they may just tell you who you are up against. This will give you the chance to compare and contrast yourself to everyone else. A clear advantage to a Stack The Deck presenter.

If you haven't established yourself as the better choice before your conclusion, don't conduct a high pressured pricing pop quiz. Asking, "How much are you looking to spend? How much did our competitor quote you?" won't get it done. Pressuring at the end and focusing on price will be your downfall. The customer's decision to buy is made long before you ask them for the order. When sales presenters use this desperate "competitor and cost tactic", it is really telling the buyer that outside of price, there is no differential value in their product.

It is important to note that most buyers will probably not divulge who else is bidding for the business anyway. Especially in a Request For Proposal (RFP) engagement. In these situations, relationships are key to discovering competitive information. You must also rely on your experience of dealing with competitors in previous deals. If you have run into companies before on similar opportunities, assume they are in the running. Build your value proposition using your strengths and against their weaknesses. I know this may sound trivial, but so many sales professionals will simply supply content from a RFP response template and insert some current data to freshen up the response. Your RFP response is exactly like your PowerPoint deck going into a presentation. Every buyer is different so take the time to customize your response. Whether it is a RFP response or closing sales presentation, the fundamentals used are the same.

Let's map out the steps needed to avoid falling into the sales equivalent of a terminal spiral. In order to close your presentation effectively, you have to plan your strategy starting with the conclusion. Decide what you want and then figure out how you are going to get there. Breaking down the anatomy of a sound closing approach brings us to our last Critical Success Factor in this book: The Assembly Line Close.

Critical Success Factor (CSF)   Bet, Raise and All-In

The Assembly Line Close

1. *Build your plan with the end in mind*

2. *Properly set your expectations for the meeting*

3. *Take the customer perspective during your presentation*

4. *Don't ask for what you haven't earned*

5. *Ask for the business*

6. *You are both your buyer's solution expert and their ambassador*

7. *Follow up and manage your next steps*

(examples and more resources are available at www.stackitonline.com and the Appendix)

Since the final moments of a presentation are really pre-determined long before it ends, **#1, "build your plan with the end in mind"** is a critical starting point when constructing your closing strategy. Preparing to close your presentation is much different than preparing to present. Your plan of action needs to be created beginning with the desired outcome then determine how to produce those results. For example, if you decided before you arrived that your goal is to leave with signed contracts, have you made sure that all necessary individuals are attending? Did you distribute the final contract to everyone before you arrive for last minute reviews? Did you conduct a pre-meeting call where you set the expectations with the customer to inform them this was the meeting's main purpose?

What if your goal is to receive an introduction to the next level in the company? Or to specific individuals that may control monetary budgets? Your actions need to establish enough credibility and confidence in you that they will sponsor you within their company. You must be aware they are judging both you and your product concurrently. Even if you had a great product, there is no guarantee you will get your meeting scheduled with the higher ups. If you arrive unprepared and rambling like a typical vendor, they may choose to do your selling for you to their superiors. In that case, they will ask you to forward your presentation materials and

Preparing to close your presentation is much different than preparing to present.

tell you to keep in touch. This happens more than you think at the corporate level to average sales people looking for advancement inside an account. Since the sponsor is tied to the sponsored, corporate employees are very selective of who they let in to see their boss. The same can be said for vendor gatekeepers. If you don't impress them, they would rather discuss your product themselves then risk a bad presenter making them look foolish for scheduling a meeting.

Each step you take in the presentation should be taking one step closer to achieving your goal. The end may be different, but how you get there should be the same. On the assembly line, you can't put the wheels on before you install the axels, so make sure you have the right parts in place before you keep going.

This leads us to **#2, "Properly set your expectations for the meeting."** It is important to be realistic in determining your meeting goals. Before you can set your expectations, you must understand everything about your potential customer. If you are entering into a sales meeting gunning for a project that won't be rolled out for another year, don't ask for the order after an hour and a half presentation. Appreciate context, buyer dynamics and other outside factors in both the industry and marketplace. For example, let's say you sell manufacturing plant inspection services and the federal government recently mandated a deadline for certain inspection data to be submitted. You should be incorporating this fact into your presentation and closing strategy. Use it as a tactic to push for a decision. Being aware of this mandate also affords you with the knowledge they have to be in compliance and therefore will need to make a decision. Other examples could be a recent influx of capital into a company, a merger and/or acquisition, lay offs or related current events. All of these outside elements directly impact your ability to achieve your end goals. Information is power and it is important to find out as much as you can before you step into your presentation.

STACK THE DECK

In most sales circles, due diligence is commonly referred to as qualifying the opportunity or customer. While I believe this is a critical process, the emphasis should first be more on you than your buyer. Instead of trying to determine if the prospect is ready to buy, you should first be concerned as to whether or not you are ready to ask for the business.

Have you considered all outside influencers like those mentioned above? Do you have your strategy set on how you are going to build a winning value proposition during the meeting? Have you set the proper expectations with your meeting attendees? This process is what I call becoming *Qualified to Close.* The answers to the questions listed below will give you a better perspective than just reading their latest press release. It will help shape your view of the buyer's entire landscape and gather valuable information to be used when asking for the business. Of course, revise this list as necessary.

1. *Are there outside factors, market trends or legislation motivating my buyer?*

2. *Is my buyer in a high growth industry and/or have their largest competitors made a similar purchase where they have to keep pace?*

3. *Has this company made previous investments related to my product or service?*
4. *Is my buyer in the midst of a restructuring, merger or acquisition that could affect their purchase timeline?*

5. *Is my buyer financially stable?*

6. *Do I have an org chart and know all the individuals involved in the project?*

7. *Who are the decision makers?*

8. *Who owns the budget?*

9. *What is my buyer's internal approval process, i.e. contracts, signatures, etc. for purchasing your product?*

10. *Who owns the delivery and ongoing management of the project from the customer side?*

11. *What is my customer's road map and future plans involving my product?*

12. *What other opportunities exist within the customer's company I can pursue at a later date once I have successfully delivered the first product?*

Once these questions have been answered, you have enough data to formulate your meeting expectations. Getting the order is the best possible outcome, but there are other positive next steps and goals to work toward in closing a presentation.

Here is a short list of possibilities I use when setting my presentation goals with number one being the best result:

1. *Signed contracts*

2. *Agreement to buy and contracts submitted*

3. *Agreement to move forward to buy, contracts requested*

4. *Agreement to move forward and buyer to consider product or service*

5. *Defined next steps and follow up*

6. Presentation failure and no defined next steps

Each one of these presentation goals above require a specific path to follow during your meeting to achieve. You must decide before you walk into your sales meeting, what you want accomplished when you leave.

You must decide before you walk into your sales meeting, what you want accomplished when you leave.

However, depending on the product or service you represent, not every presentation ends in an immediate sale. You could receive the order after one presentation or it may require multiple sales meetings. If your product is largely based on a single sales call, you don't have a chance to make up for missteps.

If your product requires a multi-step and extended sales cycle, be realistic in setting your expectations. Regardless of how many it takes, each of your sales presentations should work toward your most immediate goal. Do not try to achieve it all at once. I have seen sales reps go into an initial sales presentation working towards a win that should take months to achieve and expect a commitment at the end of the meeting. You don't get points for bravery and confidence in this context, just points deducted for making everyone feel uncomfortable. Moreover, this unrealistic outcome makes the presenter look inexperienced and desperate. Have fun trying to get invited back for a follow-up meeting.

When dealing with long sales cycles, be patient and trust your abilities. If you are using the Stack The Deck principles, the more time you have in front of your buyer should be to your advantage. Each meeting should be approached as a new presentation. Make sure you have incorporated all of your past progress, discussions and data in your presentation content. Be prepared to use it to your advantage. Think of the selling process in terms of bringing a sauce to a simmer instead of a violent boil. Smooth confidence and an even demeanor are incredibly effective. The customer is going to make a decision on their timetable, not yours. There is no need to rush them unless you are selling a life preserver to a man flailing in the water. Are you desperate for a sale or expecting to win the business? Based on how you manage your meeting and close it, your audience will know the answer.

Presentation success is not always measured in dollars and cents. Winning may mean that you at least convinced the buyer to take another step forward. Defining

There are no moral victories in sales, only wins and losses.

your expected outcome will give you an accurate benchmark to measure your achievements. Conversely, if you are proud of your effort, but somehow the customer wasn't impressed or did not agree to any positive next steps, was it really productive? There are no moral victories in sales, only wins and losses. Moral victories are claimed by weaker sales presenters not being honest with themselves on their lack of preparation and presenting skills. Don't use any other metric to gauge your presentation success then the tangible next steps and results you accomplished.

There are two sides represented in every sales presentation: you and the buyer. The only side that matters in closing the deal is the buyer's. This is why **#3, "Take the customer's perspective,"** is the next important step.

Sir Isaac Newton's third law of motion states, "For each action there is an equal and opposite reaction." Forget for a moment that this is a physics law and use it in a sales context to better understand the relationship between buyer and seller. If you want to elicit a specific *reaction* from your buyer, consider what *action* it would take for you to create it. If you were the buyer and going to award the business at the end of the presentation, what needs to take place for you to feel confident in doing that? Equally as important, what are the details and corporate requirements needed to make that happen? Most companies have a vendor application and legal process that must be followed in order to issue Purchase Orders and/or sign contracts. Moreover, if you do not properly manage and communicate with attorneys and other executives that may need to be involved, your deal could be dead before it is even submitted. Have you inquired about their specific buying guidelines and parameters?

If not, then **#4, "Don't ask for what you haven't earned"** is the best advice you can get at this point. When you set expectations for your meeting, anticipate the customer's decision criterion needed to award the business to you. For example, it is always important to involve both parties' legal and executive resources involved in the sale approval process. If you represent a "one call close" type product, then your path to a decision is considerably shorter and less layers to deal with. Remember my dot.com sales presentation debacle in chapter one? Understanding what it takes for your customer to make a decision should influence your closing strategy. If you know they need three signatures and a months worth of review in order to approve a vendor, why would you ask them to commit to the sale after a few hours? You won't get it anyway. Instead, focus on each step needed, one at a time. Show them you are committed to spending the time with them and not looking for an easy deal.

Missing these types of details will destroy your image as the subject matter expert. A buyer never wants to feel they are your first customer and that you've never done this before. As discussed earlier in this book, the buyer's own job is at risk if your product doesn't deliver. Once you have convinced them to spend their money, they have to stay convinced that their money is in good hands.

After you have satisfied all decision criterion, it is now appropriate for **#5, "Ask for the business."** Amazingly most sales presenters trip over themselves on a question that should be the easiest to ask. After all, you are at the end of your sales presentation. Your audience should already be sold, but most sales reps cannot articulate a clear argument that is compelling. I believe it is similar to a neighborhood kid who wants to mow your lawn. You agree to the price and he begins to work. A few minutes later, he doesn't finish the job, but knocks on your door to collect full payment. Is he justified in asking to get paid?

> **If you have completely sold your audience, asking for the order should be the natural next step.**

Clearly no, as there is a distinct deficit between work completed and money requested. In my opinion, herein lies the problem with typical sales people. They acknowledge, either consciously or subconsciously, that there is still considerable work to be done in convincing their buyer, yet they still push forward. Perhaps it is because every sales book tells you to go for it at the end. Maybe it is having to answer to management when you get back to the office. Regardless, the only time you should be asking for the business is when you feel you know what the answer *should* be.

As a presenter, if you have completely sold your audience, asking for the order should be the natural next step. You should expect to be writing up the contract because you believe there is no way your prospect should say, "No." Most presenters never get to this state of confidence. As mentioned many times in this book, you will never be able to control everything. I have lost sales I would have bet everything I would win and won others I thought I had lost. In sales, the unexplainable does happen, but you should expect to win every time.

This brings us to **#6, "You are both your buyer's solution expert and their ambassador."** If you have successfully utilized the Stack The Deck methods in your presentation, at the conclusion, both you and your customer are product experts. You are also a trusted advisor. Customers want to know the person who sold them is also going to be there when everything arrives. I have seen so many sales reps take a "smash and grab" approach to their accounts. Because the commission clock is running, they go in and sell hard, then run harder to their next account leaving their new customers behind. Larger companies have technical teams and operational resources that deliver the goods or services, but there is no substitute for the person that convinced them to buy in the first place.

To this point, you will derive an enormous amount of benefit from openly discussing your role in post sale activities during all your presentations. Show every audience that you are not a commission burglar. Stay involved. Take a vested interest in your customer after you get paid and talk about it as much as you can with other potential customers. You are supposed to be your customer's ambassador to your company. If they need something, it is your job to go get it. Yes, even *after* you get paid. Building this type of relationship with your customers, then constantly discussing it with other prospects will set you apart from the pack. If you can architect a solution and be there to see it to fruition, it will give you a distinct competitive advantage. Staying engaged with your customer and product delivery will also deepen your product knowledge which will pay dividends in your subsequent sales efforts.

A word of caution: you cannot be everything to everyone. Being an ambassador means you understand what is needed and know how to delegate to get it done. I personally would not feel comfortable doing business with a company where one person did it all. You can reference back to chapter 3 and **#8** in the **Character Development Critical Success Factor** for an expanded discussion as to why. Conversely, I would feel confident about a company where I knew I only had one point of contact and they would make sure it gets done on my behalf. One person to do everything or one person to contact to make sure it gets done. Do you see the difference?

If you use the techniques and strategies discussed in this book then neglect your customer afterwards, your presentation was a wasted effort. More importantly, it will cost you money in the future. A proven rule of sales is that it is easier to sell someone who already bought something from you than to sell someone something for the first time. Rarely do buyers ever make one purchase so you can count on them coming back to you if you performed well and delivered. Your customer will continue to encounter problems and need solutions so expect to be in a relationship for the long haul. If you are trying to infiltrate an account, the first questions to answer is, "Who is the incumbent?" Existing vendors are the hardest to remove from a competitive situation, especially if they are doing a great job in supporting the account. If you just sold someone your product, you are now the incumbent. Do everything you can to hold on to the account and be proactive in your relationship. Explore other business units and ask your buyers to introduce you to other individuals that may have active projects or opportunities. You will create residual revenue for your company and consistent income for you.

This brings us to **#9, "Follow up and manage your agreed upon next steps."** All of the character development, credibility and momentum you create during your presentation can be destroyed. We are all familiar with the old adage, "Actions speak louder than words." This saying could not be more accurate for a sales rep that doesn't properly follow up. How can a customer trust a *sales rep* that can't manage next steps from a *sales meeting*? They haven't even purchased anything yet and already their solution expert is mismanaging their first deliverable. Your audience took the time to listen to your presentation. The least you could do is take the time to thank them and remind them of the progress that was made. What kind of professionalism and interest are you showing to your potential customer if you do not follow through? As the sales lead, you have the responsibility of making everyone, including yourself, accountable to the agreed upon next steps.

What happens *after* the meeting should be an extension of what was agreed upon *during* the meeting. Successfully completing your post meeting activities is what I refer to as getting your *Follow Up M.B.A.* This process involves three main components which are the:

1. *Take Away Message.*

2. *Take Away Benefit.*

3. *Take Away Action.*

The first step in the *Follow Up M.B.A.* process is the *Take Away Message*. It is what you leave your audience with when you end the meeting. This really equates to your value proposition and why you have a superior product or service. We have previously discussed this many times and the message your audience takes away from your presentation is built and delivered long before the close. However, they need to be constantly reminded of this message during your follow up. This will be the common theme in all of your subsequent conversations so make sure it is clearly defined.

To illustrate this point, think of the last time you took a vacation. When I travel, I always take a lot of pictures. Photos are visual reminders of the experiences and places I visited and I love looking back at all the fun I had. Follow up discussions with your buyer should be like looking through pictures together once you return home from a vacation. Your notes and list of next steps become your proverbial pictures in your photo album. They are critical to your follow up efforts for two reasons. First, it is your job to remind your buyer of all the good that was accomplished during your presentation. Second, discussing specific details of the meeting shows your buyer that you are taking a special interest in their business. Think of the *Take Away Message* as your joint photo album with your buyer. Drag it out every time you talk with them to reconnect and remind them of what a great fit you are for their company.

The second step in getting your *Follow Up M.B.A.* is the *Take Away Benefit*. What does the customer get out of their relationship with you? Does your product solve a list of issues or increase productivity? Does your service reduce some kind of organizational problem or make life easier? Whatever you are selling, it has a benefit to the buyer and that is what you focus on. These benefits need to be well documented during the meeting because you are going to use them as a reminder of why they need to spend money with you. Benefit equals perceived value, which hopefully equals a sale.

Finally, the last step is the *Take Away Action*. A good closer will always define the next steps of a meeting before it ends. What has been agreed to? What can the customer expect from you? What can you expect from the customer? How do you go from wrapping up the meeting to achieving your next goal and expectation?

Earlier in this chapter we discussed setting meeting expectations. When you arrive at this place in your presentation, your actions should be driving two parallel efforts. Initially, you should be working toward achieving your goals set for the current meeting. Second, you should be setting yourself up for success in the next meeting if one is needed. For example, let's say you set the expectation to be sponsored to the next level with higher ranking individuals before your meeting. At your presentation close, one of the next steps discussed should be scheduling that meeting. If they are reluctant to agree to that, find out why. It may be they do not feel confident in you, your product or both. It might simply be a scheduling issue. Nonetheless, this is your chance to draw out any objections to you achieving your next step(s). Otherwise, you will be calling and emailing for follow up with no real way of telling whether or not you won them over.

People in general don't like conflict and won't tell you something negative in person if they can avoid it. Closing your meeting with discussing next steps enables you to deal with this trait head on and accomplish what you set out to do. You have the person or persons that you need in attendance, so seize the moment. They can't say they were tied up in meetings and couldn't call you back when they are sitting right in front of you.

Additionally, your Take Away Action should involve the following two steps. I know they may be obvious, but they never seem to get done in a timely manner when the meeting ends:

1. *Immediate email to all meeting participants thanking them for their time and listing out the next steps. This email may include attachments such as brochures, spec sheets, etc.*

2. *Phone call for personal follow up to the senior most attendee and the person responsible for setting the meeting.*

As you can see, successfully closing a presentation doesn't just involve shaking hands and feeling good about your meeting. It is a comprehensive process that begins long before you leave.

Chapter 6 Review

1. The Assembly Line Close

Your closing strategy should mirror the efficient process of an assembly line. By design, it produces the same result every time: a finished product. In this example, the finished product is your presentation's conclusion. In order to close your presentation effectively, you have to plan your strategy beginning with the end. Decide what you want and then figure out how you are going to get there.

2. Are You Qualified to Close?

Instead of trying to determine if the prospect is ready to buy, you should first be concerned as to whether or not you are ready to ask for the business. You need to have your strategy set on how you are going to build a winning value proposition. You can't just present and expect to win them over. You have to incorporate all outside factors and events beforehand.

3. Great Expectations

You must decide before you walk into your sales meeting what you want to accomplish before you leave. Depending on the type of product or service you represent, not every presentation may end in an immediate sale. Be sure to set realistic expectations for your presentation. Don't ask for the order if you know one is not coming anytime soon. Remember, you don't get any points for bravery.

4. Get Your Follow Up M.B.A.

All of your character development, credibility and good will you create during your presentation can be destroyed by not properly managing the post meeting activities. A sound follow up process involves three components which are the:

1. *Take Away* <u>*Message*</u>.
2. *Take Away* <u>*Benefit*</u>.
3. *Take Away* <u>*Action*</u>.

As the sales lead, you have the responsibility of making everyone, including yourself, accountable to the agreed upon next steps.

Chapter 6 Bonus Section: *Damage Control*

Stack The Deck creates confident and prepared sales professionals and is a system that will produce consistent results. It offers a great balance of public speaking, sales and presenting principles and tries to remove as many variables in a sales presentation as possible. The finished product is much like a finely tuned engine designed for high speed performance and optimal gas mileage. However, one variable that can never be removed is the sales professional. What happens when no amount of preparation or talent can save a presentation? What is the course of action to pull out of a tailspin caused solely by the presenter?

The beginning of the end for a presenter can come in many ways. Some of the most common mishaps are arriving late or failure associated with presentation software and demonstrations. While these may seem like small errors or hurdles to overcome, most sales presenters allow these events to derail their presentation and destroy their confidence.

Furthermore, most sales presenters in this situation will compound early mistakes by continuing to make them by not acting like the general on a battlefield. No matter how good you are, things will go wrong. You are in command so nothing should surprise you. If something does get you off track, pull it back in line and don't dig yourself a deeper hole.

For example, a financial services consultant was holding a luncheon at a local restaurant. She had been pursuing a large bank for some time and invited the Board of Directors to a private lunch and presentation. She waited for almost thirty minutes for them to arrive until she realized she was at the wrong restaurant. Amazingly, the Board waited for her patiently and when she finally arrived, she apologized for having a "blonde moment." Normally, this would be a humorous and acceptable excuse among friends, except this was a business meeting. Do you think a bank would trust anyone with their financial portfolios and investment strategies to anyone susceptible to a "blonde moment?" To compound the problem, the <u>blonde</u> chairwoman replied "Your hair is not even blonde, it's almost dark brown." Ouch.

I am sure having to do over again, she would have chosen a different, more professional response (like a simple apology) for mixing up the meeting location. This leads us to one of the most important rules of damage control: Don't ever throw yourself under the bus. Meaning, do not sacrifice yourself and reputation in any sales situation by somehow tying the failure to you personally or your shortcomings. I have seen this happen so many times where the presenter will forget to bring something or show up late and then apologize by saying that they "do this all the time." While this gives them the appearance of being human and normal, it severely compromises their expert status. Buyers don't want human, they want superhuman. Of course, you must be accountable for your actions and take responsibility for everything as the sales lead, but do it in a manner that suggests this type of thing does not happen very often. I am also not suggesting that you act apathetic if you show up to a meeting ten minutes late, forget to bring materials or waste everyone's time with a poor presenting performance. The decisions and statements you make in the early going dealing with adversity will greatly affect the meeting's outcome.

Small hurdles that occur in the beginning should be met with a battle tested resolve and your audience should see that nothing will throw you off course. Never break and always act like nothing can compromise the message you have for your audience. You must maintain an image of invincibility when facing any kind of trial in front of your audience. This keeps your goal in tact of establishing yourself as the expert and can also yield dividends for you later in the meeting.

We have already discussed in this book how products are never perfect. There is almost always something that goes wrong with a transaction. Whether it is shipping delays, broken parts or failed deliverables, they will be looking to you to make sure they are taken care of. Seasoned buyers know this and it is one of traits they are looking for in a vendor. Can you be counted on when things go wrong or when they are not satisfied? Handling early hurdles in a sales meeting with confidence and professionalism proves to your potential customer that you have the traits to be trusted.

Additionally, most buyers have been through countless vendor presentations so they have a lot of history in comparing your performance to others. More importantly, they have seen what negatively impacts a presenter and has caused meeting failures before. If you are able to overcome these hurdles with little or no effect, it shows that in comparison to your peers, you cannot be taken off your game. Remember, we are just starting the sales presentation and objections always come with the territory. If you cannot be rattled early when most presenters are extremely nervous, they will be filing that information away when the Q & A portion of the meeting begins. This knowledge will affect the way they ask their questions and deter grandstanders. Conversely, if they notice that your confidence is easily compromised, they have the upper hand in now knowing you do have a breaking point. "Never let them see you sweat" is a show business saying, but it is paramount you follow this advice in a sales meeting.

So there are clear advantages to you by conducting damage control during your sales presentation, but how do you do it? There are dozens of disaster scenarios that can happen and I could write an entire book on just this subject (hint). For now, I am only going to address some more common events: arriving late, presentation software failure and conducting product demonstrations. In each instance, the two most important rules to follow are to never insult yourself or use self deprecating humor and do not apologize again at the end of the meeting. If you spent the whole presentation turning a negative start into a successful conclusion, apologizing again reminds them of the rough beginning and not the great finish.

Arriving Late

If you are late, apologize and move on. Do not belabor the point and talk about how you got lost, that you are not good with directions or there was a long line at the car rental counter. These stories don't add a personal touch or in some way connect you to your audience. It doesn't matter. You were late and no amount of jibber jabber is going to change that fact. Any excuse or personal insult you make will only worsen your image and portray you as the type of person that cannot be counted on. This is early in the meeting. You want the image of strong and confident, not weak and vulnerable.

What amazes me about most sales people in this situation is that they never notify anyone they are going to be late. They hustle to the meeting then the excuses begin when they walk in the room. There is always time to make a simple phone call and/or an email if you are going to be late. If you cannot reach them by phone, send an email and call someone in your company to try to contact your buyers to let them know you are going to be late. Email is a good idea since your audience may have already arrived to a conference room having no access to their office voicemail. Someone else calling is also beneficial because it allows you to concentrate on where you are going. This has happened to me where I have compounded the problem by getting lost or missing a turn by being preoccupied with trying to call and say I was going to be late.

Secondly, always say you are going to be later than you really think you will be. Most people want to ease the initial pain of telling someone you are going to be late by minimizing the time until they arrive. It is far more painful to keep them waiting longer *after* you gave them a revised arrival time. It is double jeopardy and hard to overcome so don't cause more injury to yourself and the meeting. Give yourself more time to get there if you are going to be late and then arrive early. This technique can often offset the fact that you were late in the first place.

Presentation Software Failure

There are many presentation tools you can use: Web conferencing, Microsoft PowerPoint, Laptops and equipment. In chapter five we covered Web conferencing and how to successfully present in this environment. Unfortunately, even though this technology is mature and often used, it is prone to failure. Conversely, Microsoft's PowerPoint is extremely reliable, but laptops are not. If you are using any presenting tools, you have potential disasters lurking everywhere. Combine these issues with an Internet connection and you have a highly volatile situation.

Quick Note: One scenario, but not as severe, involves your PowerPoint not being distributed to the group. If individuals are joining via conference call and you are not using Web conferencing software, then only some of your audience can see your slides. In this context, if you have the ability to send the PowerPoint, do it immediately. If not, apologize and get their email addresses and let them know you will send it out as follow up to the meeting.

When presentation equipment and software fail, most sales presenters perform the professional equivalent of a bridge jump to end it all. They act as if the ideals, features and advantages of their company and products are locked securely away in these tools. I am only referring to presentations and not demonstrations in this section. If everything you have to say is locked away in equipment and software, do *you* really own the product you are trying to sell? Proving that you can conduct a presentation without a slide deck, especially under unexpected circumstances, gets you Hall of Fame votes in the eyes of your audience.

Product Demonstrations

If you have scheduled a Web conference to demo software and something fails to launch, end the meeting immediately. Do not keep everyone on the phone and have them listen to you struggle to get the product working that you are going to ask them to buy. Moreover, it is hard for a remote audience to determine the true root of the problem. Is it the Web conferencing software, your product or you? Don't give them time to make their own determination. Moreover, even if the problems are not related to your product, it reflects poorly on you that you cannot solve a technical problem, especially if you are selling technology. Apologize for the inconvenience, thank everyone for their time and set a time to reschedule while you have everyone together.

If you are meeting in person, demo failure is a far more serious offense. You should have been more prepared and showed up with a "plan B." Whether this means to bring an extra laptop, a wireless Internet card to connect through a wireless carrier or back up equipment, it should have been done. You cannot claim to be surprised by an unforeseen circumstance if the agenda included a demonstration. Remember constructing a Risk Assessment in chapter one? Make sure that you have accounted for every possible scenario before you arrive to present.

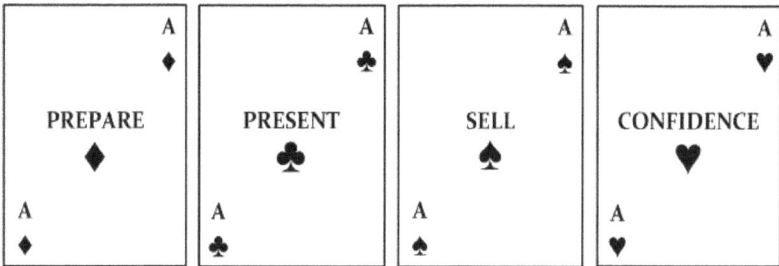

A ◆	A ♣	A ♠	A ♥
PREPARE ◆	PRESENT ♣	SELL ♠	CONFIDENCE ♥
A ◆	A ♣	A ♠	A ♥

Conclusion

When applying the principles in this book, you will start focusing more on being an effective and convincing presenter than simply surviving the meeting. If you are not on the offensive and dictating the action, you are vulnerable to whatever the buyer wants to throw at you. Moreover, you lose a valuable opportunity to prove you should be the vendor of choice while in front of the customer.

Take advantage of the fact that you can interact with your prospect and use visual clues like posture and facial expressions to know if you are on the right track.

You should own the meeting and use that time to work toward winning the sale. The customer should never have the advantage or be in control. You cannot achieve this superior position if you are not prepared. When you arrive, you should have a set agenda, know your attendees, have conducted research and customized your presenting materials. Scrambling around during the meeting looking for relevant facts or features that may sway your audience is not how you win.

Have you ever noticed how easy the last few minutes of a presentation feel? Regardless of whether or not you are going to get the business, everyone is comfortable. Why? Simple, the presenter and their team are not dealing with nerves and the unknown. When this happens, buyers and sellers become just people in a room having a conversation and discussing next steps. If you arrive prepared and ready to own the meeting, you can start how everyone else finishes. Set yourself apart through preparation and product knowledge.

If you believe in what you are selling and are genuinely excited, it is contagious.

Another benefit to this approach is that your prospect will notice that nothing makes you nervous. If you believe in what you are selling and are genuinely excited, it is contagious. Conversely, if you fumble through discussions and are overcome by nerves, weakness will affect your ability to be convincing. You are the subject matter expert and the reason for the meeting. If your buyer was going to do it themselves or had all the answers, they wouldn't need you there. Take control.

Once you have a grip on your meeting, work to establish a connection with your audience. Conquer your nerves and own your product, then you can relax and leverage your charisma and personality. You will be comfortable with driving the meeting in front of your audience. Most presenters never get to this point, which is to your advantage. Your competition will trip over themselves with shaky answers and PowerPoint® clip art. Even if you get a formidable presenting opponent, they should be no match for you given your unique ability to blend preparation, product knowledge and exceptional presenting presence.

Finally, if you are planning your closing strategy from the beginning you are already ahead of your competitors. Most sales people wait until the meeting's conclusion and then decide how to close. You must work toward your end goal from the start. How can you control the outcome if you didn't influence the steps to get there?

I encourage you to use what you've learned to your advantage to stay ahead in this fast paced sales world. Preparation and presenting skills are severely underdeveloped in today's sales culture, so I hope by reading and applying this book you have gained a competitive advantage.

Remember, no matter the amount of preparation and research, you will never have the perfect message every time. Only by owning your product and presentation will you be able to adjust and be successful in any circumstance, with any audience and any content. Preparing for everything, knowing your product and having both relevance and a connection to your audience means you now know how to Stack The Deck.

About The Author

Todd Carey is an accomplished entrepreneur, investor and executive in the mobile technology marketplace. He has founded several venture capital funded tech companies and served in a senior executive capacity in corporate business development roles. He has managed sales and technical teams as well as enterprise marketing efforts with over 13 years of industry experience. He has led multi-national sales campaigns and developed solution selling training programs.

Todd has in depth experience with international manufacturing and consulting in product development, branding and go-to-market strategies for multi-national companies. He has forged strategic alliances with Microsoft, EDS, ACNielsen, AT&T, Qualcomm, Sprint and Verizon Wireless to name a few.

He has been published in trade publications such as *Mobile Enterprise Magazine, Transaction Trends and GMA Forum.* Todd has also participated on executive panels and been a featured speaker at industry conferences.

At home, Todd has a beautiful and supporting wife, Kristin and two amazing children named Aaron and Emily. He plays basketball, tennis and golf and attends First Baptist Church in Prosper, TX.

Todd received his Bachelor's Degree in Economics from the University of Michigan.

References

1. Keri K. Stephens (2007). Making your point with PowerPoint.® In A. M. Young, & J. A. Daly (Eds.). *Professional communication skills.* Indianapolis, IN: Pearson.

2. Kathleen Katona (2004) Assistant editorial: *Stack The Deck.* Seattle, WA.

3. Nicole Geu (2007). Assistant editorial: *Stack The Deck.* Lake Zurich, IL.

4. Simon Crossley (2007). Assistant editorial: *Stack The Deck.* Plano, TX.

5. Shannon Cassidy (2007). bridge between, inc. www.bridgebetween.org. Philadelphia, PA.

STACK THE **DECK** Sales Program

Stack The Deck is one of the premier resources companies look to for empowering their sales force with sound presenting and selling fundamentals.

Now this resource can be customized to fit your company's specific products, services and selling culture though the Stack The Deck Sales Program. Compass Consulting will conduct research including sales process mapping, interview stakeholders, executives, team members and customers in order to publish a custom version of Stack The Deck for your company's employees.

Todd Carey is also available for speaking engagements at corporate events, conferences and meetings. In a highly entertaining format, he can highlight the core principles of the book or work with the executive and event planning staff to build a specific, targeted presentation for the meeting.

If you are interested in these services, please contact:

Kathleen Katona

Vice President of Marketing and Events

Compass Consulting, L.L.C.

Office: 913-702-4915

Address: 4760 Preston Road

Suite 244-249

Frisco, TX 75034

Appendix

RESOURCE CHECKLIST

COMPANY CONTACT INFORMATION	
Contact Name:	Contact Phone:
Company Address:	Meeting Date/Time:

RESOURCES I AM SUPPLYING

☐ Laptop ☐ Power Cord ☐ Demonstration Tools ☐ Printed Presentations

RESOURCES TO BE SUPPLIED

☐ Internet Connection ☐ Projector ☐ Meeting Room ☐ Building Access Card

ADMINISTRATIVE PROCEDURES

☐ Review Presentation	• Anticipate Team Questions • Commit to Memory Major Points • Time Presentation • Business cards • APK up to par	• Meet w/your team prior to meeting

STACK THE DECK

RESOURCE CHECKLIST (CONT.)

☐ Introductions to team.

☐ Review Product Purchase plans.

☐ Review expectations and standards.

☐ Review schedule.

☐ Review timelines.

TECHNICAL REQUIREMENTS

☐ Review any technical requirements

DEVELOPING ADAPTIVE PRODUCT KNOWLEDGE

INTERNAL QUESTIONNAIRE- TO COMPANY REPRESENTATIVE

What is your role(s) within the company?

How long have you been working in this specific area?

What are the greatest strengths of our company?

Can you give me an overview of our product/service?

What are the important features of our product?

Who is involved in building and maintaining our product/service?

What steps do we take to prepare to deliver our product/service?

What are the areas we should target for product/service improvement?

What do you think our customers say about us to others?

What company resources and documentation are available for research?

STACK THE DECK

INTERNAL QUESTIONNAIRE- TO COMPANY REPRESENTATIVE

Who else do you recommend
I speak with in the company?

DEVELOPING ADAPTIVE PRODUCT KNOWLEDGE

EXTERNAL QUESTIONNAIRE- TO CUSTOMER

What is your role(s) within the company?

How long have you been working in this specific area?

How long have you been working with our product/service?

In what business area do you use our product/service?

What are the most important features of our product to you?

Who is involved from your company in maintaining our product/service

Can you describe how we delivered our product/service to you?

How successful was the delivery?

How do we support you today?

What do you think are the biggest strengths of our product/service?

What are the areas we should

STACK THE DECK

EXTERNAL QUESTIONNAIRE- TO CUSTOMER

target for improvement as a company?

What are the areas we should target for product/service improvement?

What would you say if another customer asked about us?

CREATING A STORY BOARD

STORY BOARD SUMMARY

☐ Content will be defined by your meeting strategy

☐ Start with a general discussion such as an overview or recap

☐ Narrow your focus so your content moves more in line with your meeting strategy

☐ The final presentation slides are your most specific content and dedicated to closing the meeting as you have defined

Answer the questions on the left, then follow the examples on the right:

	Example 1:	Example 2:
1. What do you want to accomplish in this meeting?	1. Introduce our company and products to a potential customer.	1. Convince the prospect to select our company with a final presentation before a buying decision is made.
2. Decide on the meeting content that will be discussed in order to achieve your goals.	2. The new cleaning products and the improvements we have made to our warranty programs.	2. Recap the sales cycle, testing or evaluation results and why the prospect should select our company.
3. Begin with the most general subject matter to start the meeting.	3. Who we are as a company and our current customers.	3. Begin with a

Insert the value proposition. 4. **Continue to narrow your focus and discussion through each slide, getting to the most important content that needs to be discussed.**	Insert value proposition. 4. Industry overview of what the latest advancements are in cleaning products. The specific features of our cleaning products. Why our product line is superior.	timeline and overview of the sales effort that has been made. Remind them of our value proposition. 4. Strong closing statements as to why we deserve to win the business.

www.ingramcontent.com/pod-product-compliance
Lightning Source LLC
Chambersburg PA
CBHW031941190326
41519CB00007B/611